CHRISTMAS
2014

for Jim O'

from

RUTH & JOHN

CHRISTMAS

ALSO BY DR. JOE PARENT

Zen Golf: Mastering the Mental Game

ZEN PUTTING

Mastering the Mental Game on the Greens

DR. JOE PARENT

GOTHAM
BOOKS

GOTHAM BOOKS

Published by Penguin Group (USA) Inc.

375 Hudson Street, New York, New York 10014, U.S.A.

Penguin Group (Canada), 90 Eglinton Avenue East, Suite 700, Toronto, Ontario, M4P 2Y3, Canada (a division of Pearson Penguin Canada Inc.); Penguin Books Ltd, 80 Strand, London WC2R 0RL, England; Penguin Ireland, 25 St Stephen's Green, Dublin 2, Ireland (a division of Penguin Books Ltd); Penguin Group (Australia), 250 Camberwell Road, Camberwell, Victoria 3124, Australia (a division of Pearson Australia Group Pty Ltd); Penguin Books India Pvt Ltd, 11 Community Centre, Panchsheel Park, New Delhi – 110 017, India; Penguin Group (NZ), 67 Apollo Drive, Mairangi Bay, Auckland 1311, New Zealand (a division of Pearson New Zealand Ltd); Penguin Books (South Africa) (Pty) Ltd, 24 Sturdee Avenue, Rosebank, Johannesburg 2196, South Africa

Penguin Books Ltd, Registered Offices: 80 Strand, London WC2R 0RL, England

Published by Gotham Books, a division of Penguin Group (USA) Inc.

First printing, April 2007

5   7   9   10   8   6   4

Gotham Books and the skyscraper logo are trademarks of Penguin Group (USA) Inc.

LIBRARY OF CONGRESS CATALOGING-IN-PUBLICATION DATA

Parent, Joseph.

Zen putting : mastering the mental game on the greens / Joe Parent.

p.   cm.

Includes bibliographical references and index.

ISBN-13: 978-1-592-40267-0 (hardcover)   1. Putting (Golf)—Psychological aspects.

I. Title.

GV979.P8P29 2007

796.352'35—dc22   2006027208

Printed in the United States of America

Set in Filosofia with Gill Sans

To my teachers,
who showed me the way to help others learn,
and to my students,
from whom I keep learning more and more.

CONTENTS

PART 3
Training Your Mind   39

PART 4
How to Make Every Putt   65

PART 7
Getting Out of Your Own Way   157

PART 8
Golf and Life:
Putting Things into Perspective   185

ACKNOWLEDGMENTS

There are many people to whom I am grateful for their contribution to the development of this book. Whatever wisdom may be expressed in this work is what I learned from my teachers, the Venerable Chögyam Trungpa Rinpoche, and the Vajra Regent Ösel Tendzin (Thomas F. Rich), as well as many other great masters of mind and meditation with whom I have had the privilege of studying, including the current holder of their lineage of practice and study, Trimê Lhawang (Patrick Sweeney). A special thank you to my Zen archery (*kyudo*) teachers, Kanjuro Shibata Sensei XX, Imperial Archer and Bowmaker of Japan, and his main disciple, Sam West. They show what it means to never give up and never give in.

Although we now live far apart, I will always be grateful to my dear friend and fellow coach, Ed Hanczaryk, one of Canada's top fifty teaching professionals. It was his encouragement and conviction that I had something very unique to offer that inspired my career path.

There can't be a teacher without students or a coach without players. To the many golfers who were willing to think outside the box and entrusted their games to our work together, I am deeply grateful. Much appreciation to Vijay Singh, who recognized and applied what *Zen Golf* had to offer in his climb to number one in the world, as well as many other touring professionals, including David Toms, Len Mattiace, Carlos Franco, Tim Petrovic, Steve Lowery, Wes Short, Jr., Doug Barron, Jason Schultz, Jon Fiedler, David Berganio, Jr., Mhairi McKay, Brian Wilson, Mike Meehan, Tommy Barber, Jr., and all the other tour players with whom I've worked and made friendships over the years.

Thanks to my colleagues, other coaches who have shared their insights and inspirations, including Fran Pirozzolo, Fred Shoemaker, Dave LiCalsi, David Leadbetter, Jim Flick, Eddie Merrins, Rob Akins, Tom Barber, Michael Hunt, Katherine Roberts, Glen Albaugh, Tina Mickelson, Steve DiMarco, and many others. To Jack and Barbara Nicklaus, much appreciation—to Jack for the inspiration of his unsurpassed mental game, to Barbara for her unsurpassed graciousness and kindness.

To Michael Murphy, Steve Cohen, and the members of the Shivas Irons Society, appreciation for their genuine love of the beauty and mystery of golf, and for inviting me into their clan.

To Mark Greenslit, Jeff Johnson, and all the staff at the Ojai Valley Inn & Spa Resort in Ojai, California, and to Kirk Reese, Jim Schaeffer, Erik Evans, and all the staff and members of The Los Angeles Country Club, thank you for welcoming me to teach at such marvelous golf courses and learning facilities.

Thanks to many dear friends who have supported and encouraged my work over the years: Edward Sampson, Glen Kakol, Lyle Weinstein, Kathryn Butterfield, Randy Sunday, Ladye Eugenia Stewart, Avilda Moses, Jim and Diana Torbert, David Yossem, and many more. Thanks to the Ojai Valley Dharma Center and other meditation centers who supported and encouraged my work in teaching golf as a vehicle for practicing mindful awareness and manifesting true warriorship.

Thanks to some new friends who have been willing to lend their celebrity to help increase awareness of my teaching, including Ray Romano, Kevin James, Malcolm McDowell, Rick Dees, Kenny G, Oscar De La Hoya, Michael O'Keefe, and others.

Thanks to the coaches who helped with many Zen Golf programs over the years that served as the source for many of the lessons in this book, especially Steve Moore, Lee Woodard, and Mark Henry.

Thanks to Ryan Judkins, Kerry Perl, Gavin Lee, Tom Moretti and Mark Moore for helping me share these teachings with the corporate world.

To golf writers Jaime Diaz, Guy Yocom, Tim Rosaforte, Scott Smith, Michael Arkush, and others, many thanks for making my work known to a wider audience.

Many thanks to my publisher, Bill Shinker, and my editor, Hilary Terrell, of Gotham Books, for their vision, guidance, and support. Great appreciation to my literary agent, Angela Rinaldi. She is a very special person and close friend who inspired me in many ways to complete this work. Angela, you're still the best. Continued appreciation to Jason Kaufman, an accomplished editor who helped shape my first book.

I am very grateful to wordsmith and golf partner Ken Zeiger for generously putting his time and energy into going over the manuscript with me again and again to make it the best it could be.

Last but not least, deep gratitude to my whole family for their encouragement in my work on this book. Mom and Dad, my sister, Nancy, and my brother, Jack, have all been tremendously supportive and encouraging of my teaching and writing. Nan, a wonderful writer herself, always helps me remember that I have no idea how fortunate I have been.

Whatever has not been presented clearly in this book is my responsibility alone. Any insights or benefit that have come from this work is due solely to the kindness of my teachers.

INTRODUCTION

How you start anything depends on where you're heading, and the ultimate intention of golf is to get the ball into the hole. In the same way, the Zen tradition regards the goal as the foundation of the path. If we don't know how to finish, what is the point in starting? That's why, for golfers of all levels, I always start our lessons with putting.

As much as our state of mind affects our putting, it's also true that our putting reveals our state of mind. The insights we gain about putting allow us to make strokes that are more committed, trusting, and free. That will naturally start to become the way we play all our shots. Conversely, the mental obstacles we encounter in putting are likely to cause us interference that can affect the rest of our game. Overcoming such obstacles is the key to breaking through to lower scores. The stories and lessons in *Zen Putting: Mastering the Mental Game on the Greens* are about freeing ourselves from fear and doubt, and activating the most important element in putting: confidence.

Putting is often spoken of as its own game within the game of golf. It is the one aspect of the game that is intentionally played along the ground. There are different sets of rules that apply only on the putting green. In putting, you see the greatest variety of implements and techniques for executing exactly the same shot.

Putting is as much an art as it is a technical skill. It requires no special strength, speed, size, or dexterity. While few can hit a drive with the ability of a top professional, almost anyone has the capability to stroke a putt as well as the best. Because the putting stroke is a simpler motion than the full swing, the mental game is a greater factor in determining success or failure in putting than in any other type of golf shot.

The closer one gets to the hole in playing a shot, the more pressure there is to finish well. A poor drive can be remedied by a great approach shot; a poor approach can be remedied by a great chip shot. There is no remedy for a missed four-foot putt. In golf, the putting green is where the ultimate drama of victory versus defeat unfolds. A pressure-packed putt holds the potential for either the most frustrating or the most rewarding feeling you can have at the end of a hole, a round, or a tournament.

What does Zen have to do with putting? Zen is both the path and the goal. It is the state of mind that is completely present, completely aware, completely balanced. It is also the practice that leads to a more and more continuous experience of that state of mind. The qualities of Zen are exactly what are needed for peak performance in putting: panoramic perspective and one-pointed focus, ease and intensity, balance and poise, and above all—fearless confidence.

I've written *Zen Putting* for two reasons. One is to help golfers get out of their own way and excel at putting. It is painful to see anxiety, doubt, fear, and defensiveness paralyze a golfer before a crucial putt. Frustration, anger, and self-loathing often erupt after a missed putt. Misery, irritation, and resignation can take hold in a deeper way over a period of time when golfers struggle with their putting. Putting evokes these emotions more than any other aspect of golf because it seems the simplest and therefore is the most disappointing when there's failure. It is my hope that the lessons in this book can lessen that pain.

I also hope these lessons can help more golfers experience the joy of putting: the intuitive knowing of the path for the putt, the ease that comes with confidence in one's stroke, the wonderful feeling of the sweet spot contacting the ball, and the excitement of watching that beautifully struck putt roll steadily on its way as if it were seeking the hole with a mind of its own.

The other and more important reason for this book is to help people get out of their own way and better enjoy their lives. Putting is a microcosm of golf, and golf is a microcosm of life. As the saying goes, "It is possible that golf builds character. It is certain that golf reveals character." How we relate to our experiences on the golf course, and putting in particular, gives us a window into the way we are likely to relate to any other circumstances in life. I hope that the principles and methods presented in *Zen Putting* will benefit you in your golf game and in the way you experience your whole life.

The techniques you'll be shown in *Zen Putting: Mastering the Mental Game on the Greens* are based on the same core principles presented in my first book, *Zen Golf*. You'll be introduced to a unique perspective that applies modern psychology and the ancient wisdom of the Buddhist and martial arts traditions to the mystery of putting. *Zen Putting* evolved from my work with top golf professionals as well as amateurs of all levels, from beginner to state champion.

Tiger Woods said in a television interview, "My mother's a Buddhist. In Buddhism, if you want to achieve enlightenment, you have to do it through meditation and self-improvement through the mind. That's something she's passed on to me: to be able to calm myself down and use my mind as my main asset."

The Buddhist tradition is known as the Middle Way, the path that is free from extremes of attitudes and actions. The ideal state is not something that can be put into words. In the same way, the Zone in golf can be described only by what it is not. It is free from the extremes of hope and fear, past and future, worry and carelessness. *Zen Putting* uses the principle of the Middle Way to teach you how to be centered and present in body and mind, not veering too much one way or the other.

Language is a major theme that pervades *Zen Putting*. Our language expresses our views, thoughts, attitudes, feelings, and intentions. It reveals the qualities of our self-concepts: how we think about ourselves and see ourselves on the golf course, and how we suppose others see us. In *Zen Putting* you'll learn the kinds of language that are most helpful and unhelpful for better putting, as well as for the way you play the game of golf and live your life. You'll be able to choose the self-talk that works best for you to reinforce positive attitudes and diminish negativity.

Zen Putting is different from most books on putting. It is not an instruction manual of technical data and personality profiles, nor a complex step-by-step system that you have to follow from beginning to end. *Zen Putting* is a collection of brief but potent chapters offering the wisdom of traditional Zen stories and teachings applied in actual lessons with golfers, including many touring professionals. You can move from one chapter to another depending on your needs and interests, letting you find your personal path to confidence in putting.

The lessons in *Zen Putting* include methods for working with thoughts and emotions; for settling, centering, and synchronizing your body and mind; and for changing unhelpful habits. You'll find easy-to-understand sets of exercises, drills, and routines that you can draw on to take your game to the next level. Applied properly, the techniques in *Zen Putting* will help you achieve balance, focus, and confidence, the core mental states for optimum performance.

In reading this book, please remember that it is written on paper, not in stone. The techniques are intended to facilitate your growth, to offer you possibilities to explore. What works for one person may not be the best for another. Although the principles of how the mind runs the body are completely universal, the ideal combination of methods for applying those insights to your situation is entirely unique.

The opening sections of *Zen Putting* explore the meaning of confidence, the ideal state of mind for achieving excellence in putting, in all of golf, and in life. You'll discover what interferes with experiencing confidence, largely a matter of getting in your own way. You'll learn the perspectives and the mindful awareness practices that allow you to train your mind like you train your body, to overcome those obstacles and achieve peak performance.

The central sections of *Zen Putting* teach you "how to make every putt," and how to get the most out of your game. Once you are in the proper state of mind, you can apply yourself more successfully to the fundamentals of reading greens and executing your best putting stroke time after time. You'll be given instruction on how to change from worrying about results to delighting in executing your process. There will be explanations of how to warm up properly before your round and how to develop a good routine, a smooth stroke, commitment to path, and feel for pace—all the aspects that combine to get the ball rolling and heading for the hole. You'll also learn some special techniques that will help you deal with challenging situations on and around the greens.

The last sections of *Zen Putting* focus on learning, practice, and improvement. You'll discover how to turn your game around when things aren't going well, get the most out of lessons, be your own coach, and structure your practice sessions. You'll learn a simple but highly effective technique for changing unhelpful habit patterns into useful, positive, and repeatable actions. Finally, we'll look at the ways in which you can take the lessons learned on the putting green and apply them to the rest of your game and the rest of your life. Many of my students tell me that what they learn from my coaching is as important to them in their lives as in their golf.

It is my hope that this book will help you to discover your unconditional confidence, to rouse your curiosity about what may be holding you back and how you can go beyond imagined limits, and to feel all the excitement and joy there is waiting for you in putting, in golf, and in life.

ZEN
PUTTING

PART I

Unconditional Confidence

Confidence is a change in attitude that makes the seemingly unworkable workable. This doesn't mean that all of a sudden everything is going to go our way. But it does mean that we can appreciate life even when things don't go our way. We have the resources to live in the challenge. That is the expression of courage.

—Venerable Chögyam Trungpa,
Shambhala: The Sacred Path of the Warrior

Imaginary Golf

Two friends decided they would dedicate their round of golf that day just to practicing their mental game. They went out to the course without any equipment, planning to visualize every shot, playing with imaginary clubs and balls. On the first tee, one stood up, took his stance, and made a swing with his imaginary club. "Two eighty, right down the middle," he proclaimed. Then the other fellow stepped forward and made his swing. "Two ninety, center of the fairway," he responded.

Out on the fairway, both announced the imaginary iron shot they would play, swung, and described how close to the hole their imaginary ball landed on the green. Each imagined their putt going straight into the hole for birdie.

Naturally, they made birdies and eagles all the way around and found themselves standing in the fairway of the eighteenth hole, the score all-square.

"I believe I'm away," said one of them. "I've got about one fifty to the pin, and I think it's an eight-iron." He took his stance, swung his imaginary eight-iron, pointed toward the green, and exclaimed, "It's heading for the flag . . . it's rolling toward the hole . . . it's in the hole!"

His friend calmly said, "Too bad. You lose."

"What do you mean? I just holed out!"

"You hit my ball."

Of course, we don't play imaginary golf; we use real clubs and balls. The mental game is not something separate and independent of the physical reality of our equipment, our body, and the environment of the golf course. The key to the mental game is how our mind and body work together in the action of the moment.

You can't play golf without a body, and you can't play golf without a mind. The problem is, too often they are working at cross-purposes. We need to synchronize body and mind to maximize our performance.

Our body responds to images from our mind. Different things can interfere with a single clear image, leaving the body in a state of confusion. There may be mixed messages of hope and fear, multiple images coexisting because of a lack of commitment to one intention, or distractions that leave us with no image at all. When your mind commits to one clear image, your body will do its best to produce that result.

The body is always in the present. When the mind is in the present, not preoccupied with thoughts about the last shot or the next one, then body and mind are synchronized. Understand the ways your body and mind work best together and you'll play your best golf.

Just Don't Know

In *Zen Golf*, I presented a traditional description of different kinds of students, represented by four cups in different conditions: (1) upside down, so nothing is heard; (2) having a hole in the bottom, so nothing is retained; (3) coated with dirt, so everything taught gets polluted; and (4) upright, solid and clean, so that what is taught is received properly for learning.

The Zen saying "just don't know" is the antidote to the inter-ference and pollution experienced by the third kind of stu-dent, the one who brings along his or her own preconceptions and prejudices.

"Just don't know" means setting aside what you think you know, clearing out any opinion. It is an attitude that allows you to think outside the box, because you aren't limited by expec-tations or biases. Entering into every situation with an open mind, you don't prematurely close off possibilities.

Zen means waking up to the present moment, being open to information, holding no fixed ideas. The Zen mind per-ceives this moment exactly as it is, things as they are rather than preconceived notions of how things should be. When we "just don't know," we are not on guard against informa-tion that threatens our way of understanding our world, be-cause we are not stuck in a closed-minded view of what we encounter.

What we usually refer to as beginner's luck is a successful result that happens when someone doesn't know how difficult a particular shot is supposed to be, or what could go wrong in a situation. That is an expression of "just don't know."

Usually veteran pros have the advantage of experience in playing the same course year after year in a given tournament. I was congratulating a regular on tour for winning a tourna-ment played at a new course. He said, "It wasn't so hard. I didn't know where the trouble was."

Are You a River
or a Statue?

Would you rather be a river or a statue? A river is flowing, liquid; a statue is static, solid. A river is constantly changing; a statue is always the same.

When that question is posed to the participants in one of my golf or business programs, most everyone says, "River." However, the way we usually think of ourselves, the image we have, more closely resembles a statue. We see ourselves in a particular way at this point in time, and project that view of ourselves into the past and the future. We have a name for the current version of who we think we are. In fact, we have three names: "Me, Myself, and I."

Is today's version of "me" the same as the "me" of twenty years ago? As the "me" of five years ago? As "me" last year? Is it exactly how I saw myself yesterday? An hour ago? Ten minutes ago?

In fact, there is no way to actually stay the same over time. We are continually changing. Holding on to a version of ourselves that doesn't change only serves to keep us stuck in our habitual patterns, less and less responsive to what the world has to offer.

We are also likely to see others as unchanging entities. When we see a person we know, we expect her to be a particular way rather than wondering what she'll be like today. We could take a fresh, curious view of others rather than assume that they'll be the same as the last time we saw them.

It's safer to be a statue. When you are the same every day, there's a certain security. As a golfer, it's comfortable to shoot about the same score each time. In fact, when we start to play particularly well, anxiety often arises. Fearing that we can't keep it up, we wonder when the usual screwup will start. All too often we relieve the anxiety by a three-putt, which brings an outward show of frustration but often an inner relief of staying in a certain comfort zone. "Yes, there I go again. That's what I expected." That good old recognizable "me."

The problem with statues is that although they are reliable, they never grow. If something doesn't move or change or grow, it isn't really alive. A river is much more alive than a statue. A river nourishes and accommodates lots of living things. A statue is a resting place for pigeons, and suffers the inevitable consequence.

Although you can identify a particular river by name and general location, it never stays the same. It is continually moving and different at every point of its journey. If you see yourself more that way—less solid, less limited, able to be a different person in different circumstances—you won't be so attached to how things are nor need so much for things to come out a particular way. You'll be more flexible, responsive, and open to new ideas and experiences. Being this way allows you to continually grow and evolve. It's more challenging, but also more rewarding, to be a river.

Unconquerable Confidence

Many years ago, a great general prepared his troops for a crucial battle. He felt that his strategy and his soldiers' skill were superior to that of the enemy, and therefore his troops would be victorious. However, his army was outnumbered two to one and his men were worried that they would not be able to overcome those odds. The general knew that victory depended on his soldiers' fearless confidence; entering into a battle with fear and doubt guaranteed defeat.

Just before reaching the battlefield, they stopped to prepare themselves. The general called all the soldiers into formation and announced that he had been given a message from his teacher, a great Zen master.

"My teacher has told me to toss a gold coin high in the air while all of you think of the coming battle. If the coin lands with tails showing, you will lose the battle, turn tail and run in defeat. If the coin lands heads up, you will win the battle and your heads will be held high in victory. Watch and learn your destiny."

The general threw the coin high in the air. All the men gasped and held their breath as they thought of the upcoming battle. The coin landed heads up, and a great cheer arose from the troops. Brimming with confidence, they charged the enemy forces and routed them easily.

After the battlefield was secured, the general gathered his commanders together. One of them congratulated him on the victory, adding, "Of course, our strategy had little to do with it. The coin toss revealed our destiny, and so the outcome was settled before the battle even began."

"So it was," said the general, as he showed them his gold coin that had heads on both sides.

Confidence in putting is a feeling of certainty that you can get the job done, a positive attitude that the putt is headed for the hole. Confident putting is free from doubt and anxiety, free from the hesitation and tension that accompany fear and pessimism.

For most people, confidence comes and goes. That is conditional confidence, and is based on recent results. It depends on information from a relatively short period of time. It is temporary and fluctuates, because it is determined by whatever success or failure you've experienced in the last few holes. Conditional confidence is like asking your putter after each hole, "What have you done for me lately?"

When we hole a few putts, we feel more confident, and think that we are putting well. We trust our stroke and swing the putter freely. More short putts go in; more long ones come very close if they don't drop. When we feel good about our putting, we pay more attention to the ones we hole than the ones we don't.

However, when we miss a few in a row that we think we should have holed, we feel less confident, and start to doubt our ability. We second-guess our read, doubt our stroke technique, and make more hesitant swings. We start missing short putts and start three-putting from long range. When we feel self-conscious and insecure about our putting, we pay more attention to the ones we miss, and regard as lucky any that get into the hole, seemingly in spite of ourselves.

Unconditional confidence means taking a bigger perspective, independent of moment-to-moment results. Unconditional confidence is less an expression of certainty about the outcome than a deeply held belief that you can handle whatever happens. Unconditional confidence includes a feeling of contentment about your ability to meet the challenges you are facing. How you feel about yourself need not depend on how your last putt turned out.

Unconditional confidence in your putting means that you believe you are a great putter, even if you've made a few poor putts. You see good putts as a confirmation of your fundamental ability; you regard poor putts as flukes, the result of temporary conditions or distractions. The same principle applies to your whole game. You have the choice of seeing yourself as a good golfer who has hit some poor shots, or as a poor golfer who gets lucky once in a while. It's up to you. As the great industrialist Henry Ford said: "Believe you can or believe you can't, either way you're right."

The most profound level of unconditional confidence is an underlying belief in your own worthiness as a person, beyond putting, beyond golf, beyond any circumstances of your life. It is unshakable trust in your basic goodness as a human being.

When you have the panoramic view of unconditional confidence, you can evaluate what is happening in any situation from an unbiased vantage point. There will be a more accurate reflection of reality because you can see things in their own terms. There is no need to see things in a one-sided way based on a desire for confirmation or to build up your self-esteem. Openness to experience without bias provides you accurate, valuable information for learning and improving your process for the future. You know what works fine just the way it is, what you need to develop or enhance, and what you need to refrain from or change. Clarity of purpose and commitment to action naturally arise from the firm ground of unconditional confidence.

Already in the Hole

During a practice round before a major tournament, Vijay and Paul were both on the green with birdie putts. Paul was about twenty-five feet away; Vijay had a fifteen-footer. Paul said playfully, "You'd better get ready to make yours, because mine's going in." Vijay responded, "Yours better go in, because mine's *already* in. In my mind, I already holed it." Paul holed his putt, and then Vijay rolled his in as well, just as he had envisioned it.

Many golfers have experienced intuitively knowing that a putt, particularly a somewhat long and breaking putt, was going to go in. It is a moment when you feel you know the future. It is as if it practically doesn't matter how you stroke the putt—with your eyes closed, standing backward, with one hand—there is no way that it is *not* going in the hole. It's a feeling of certainty, a combination of calm and intensity, a little glimpse of being in the Zone.

Everything seems simple. You don't have to figure out the way the putt will break; you just see it. You feel naturally at ease and focused at the same time, not in any way trying to concentrate, but already being present, without any distraction. It can happen even in the midst of intense competition. Those are amazing moments. They let you know there's something much bigger and more profound than this little thinking mind.

Those feelings of certainty and calm are not something you can manufacture. They come to you from your intuition, your instinct. You can't crank them up from your thinking, self-conscious, directing mind. Yet you can invite them by lay-ing the ground, creating the atmosphere, which allows them to arise more easily. One way to do so involves visualization. As in the story above, the best visualization is seeing the ball as already having rolled into the hole. Seeing in your mind's eye that the putt has been completed, with the ball already in the hole, means there is no need to *try* to get it in the hole. You may even feel that there are so many different ways the putt could fall in that you can trust it to find its way. That leaves you free to let your body execute your process without trying too hard, without being overly careful—in other words, without your thinking mind getting in the way.

Zen Putting is about maintaining an attitude and committing to a routine that allows your mind to be free of the interference that obstructs your intuition. By focusing on the process of putting without attachment to results, you connect with the unconditional confidence out of which certainty about a particular putt arises.

Practicing in this way, your confidence and trust will increase. The more you develop trust in yourself, rely on unconditional confidence in your ability, and let your instincts take over, the more often that feeling of certainty will come to you. It is exactly the joyful way that children play, and a wonderful way for everyone to play the game of golf.

Always in the Zone

Long ago there was a man who was very suspicious of others. He didn't trust banks to keep his money, so he always bought gold coins *and kept them hidden from prying eyes by burying them in a bag in his yard at night when no one could see. If he needed money for his expenses, he dug them up at night, took out one or two coins, and then reburied the bag in a different place.*

One night he dreamt that a neighbor saw him bury his coins. Fearful they would be stolen, he dug them up again and took them into the mountains to hide them more securely. He found an un-usual rock formation as a landmark and buried the coins near it. His dream ended with him going home, getting into bed, and falling asleep.

Several days later, he needed to buy something. He thought, "Let's see, where was the last place I buried my bag of gold coins? Oh yes, by that special rock formation in the mountains." His dream was so realistic that he had forgotten it was a dream.

He went up into the mountains, taking care that no one was following him, and went to where he remembered the rock forma-tion to be. It wasn't there. He looked in another direction. Not there either. He spent the whole day looking but couldn't find the land-mark, still not realizing that he had only imagined it in his dream.

Heartbroken, he headed home. For years he went to the moun-tains to look for his gold, but always came home empty-handed. He felt like a poor man who had lost his riches, although they were there in his own backyard the whole time.

The Zone is that magical state of being in which you have sharp focus and panoramic vision, a deep sense of ease and confi-dence, and freedom from fear. Most of what is written about finding the Zone includes recognizing only what it's like when you're in the Zone or what prevents you from being in the Zone. There is nothing telling you how to find the Zone. There's a reason no one can tell you how to find the Zone. That's because

it isn't something you can find. It isn't something that's missing. It isn't something separate from you. You can't find it *because you never lost it*.

Not only is each and every one of us always in the Zone, it is
in fact our innate state of being. It is our natural state of mind,
continuously present as the background of all we do. The only
reason we don't experience it all the time is because we wander
around, like the man in the story, mistakenly looking for it as
something we've lost. Trying to possess it gets in the way of experiencing it.

That's why good golfers who are struggling often have the
intuition that they would be playing great golf if they could just
get out of their own way. Trying to use our mind in a way that
attempts to control the body, as if they were separate, blocks
our experience of the Zone. Since the Zone is the natural syn-
chronization of our body and mind, anything we do that treats
it otherwise is interference that diminishes our optimum performance. When we get out of our own way, we are doing things
naturally, and feel like we're in the Zone. We will experience
the Zone any time there is an absence of interference from
mistaken thinking and emotional upheaval.

Like the sun hidden behind the clouds, the Zone is merely
obscured by interference, not eliminated by it. When the clouds
part, the sun doesn't have to try to shine; its rays are constantly
available whenever there are no clouds blocking them. In the
same way, the experience of the Zone doesn't have to be man-
ufactured; the feeling of ease and confidence is our natural
state that emerges whenever the clouds of confusion and negativity are cleared.

That we are always in the Zone, that it is our inherent
natural state, is a cornerstone of *Zen Putting*. Taking this particular approach to working with mind and behavior means

that we regard our optimum performance as our baseline. In the absence of interference, we will consistently play our best. How good our best is depends on the extent to which we've trained in the skills to be performed, and developed the stamina and strength to perform them. Start with the confidence that you possess the highest level of physical and mental ability for which you have trained. Remember that you are naturally capable of performing at that level, and it is only interference of one sort or another that keeps your best from showing up time after time.

Take a Step Back

Richie, a tour pro, was down on himself when he called me. He'd had a bad couple of months. "I'm just a chump," he said, "a real hacker."

I asked him to stand with his face two inches from the wall.

"How much of the room can you see?" I asked.

"Not a whole heck of a lot," he said. I told him to take a step back, and asked him the same question. He said he could see more, but still just that wall. After three more steps back, he could see most of the room.

"You've been looking at your game, but only seeing the last few months," I told him. "Take a few steps back like you did from the wall, get some perspective on your accomplishments and your talent, and you can see how well you've done over the long term."

He told me about his many victories spanning the years all the way back to championships in junior golf. After just a few minutes, he said, "You know, you're right. When I think about all that I've done in the last fifteen years instead of just dwelling on the last few months, I feel like I'm a heck of a good golfer."

Taking a step back means looking at the situation from a bigger perspective. We all go through ups and downs, experiencing them in the course of a day, a month, a year, or a career. Dwelling on bad feelings when you are down can make you forget that you ever felt good about your game.

Our memories are short. If you've had a cold for a long time, near the end you start feeling a little better but not one hundred percent. You wonder if this sort-of-okay feeling is as good as it gets.

It's like that when you're going through a dry spell in putting. You find yourself in a slump, thinking, "Maybe this is as good as I can putt," and you start to become resigned to that level, not remembering how much better you were in the past.

Looking at your experience through a wider lens helps you to see beyond your current circumstances and get a breath of fresh air. When you look at the big picture, it liberates you from the small-minded funk you find yourself caught in. You are more open to making an objective review of your putting routine and how your stroke feels. You may find an unnoticed old tendency getting in the way and remember a simple remedy. It is easier to reconnect with unconditional confidence in your capabilities and realize your full potential when you take a step back.

Tough Course

The CEO of a company played golf very rarely, and wasn't very good at it. Each year at the annual company outing, the employees would beg him to join them in the golf tournament. Each year he found a reason to decline. Finally, he ran out of reasons and excuses, and agreed to play.

The day of the tournament came. He was first on the tee. The whole company gathered around. He stood to address the ball, made a little waggle, and then a full swing. Whoosh. He had whiffed, missed it completely. He gathered himself, stepped back up to the ball, waggled, and swung. Whoosh. The ball was still sitting there on the tee. A murmur passed through the crowd of employees. He composed himself again, took a practice swing, and addressed the ball a third time. He took a big swing and topped the ball along the ground, just onto the forward tee.

The CEO reflected a moment, then turned around to the gathered onlookers and said, "Whew! Tough course!"

That's an example of a great sense of humor. True humor isn't dependent on laughs at someone else's expense, nor being overly self-deprecating. It is an expression of the absence of self-importance. It is not taking oneself or one's project too seriously, and so expresses an atmosphere of lightness and enjoyment.

Not taking oneself too seriously on the golf course means having expectations that are in line with the situation. Unrealistic expectations cause a great amount of frustration and therefore a lack of humor and enjoyment. Great golfers don't hit every fairway, don't hit every green, don't chip it close every time, and don't make every putt. How often they do accomplish those feats is a tribute to the amount that they practice and play: years of practice, thousands of range balls, hundreds of rounds. Their handicap is scratch or better. So if you are a fifteen-handicap who doesn't play or practice nearly as much as a tour pro, why are you so frustrated and surprised when you miss a fairway or green, or lip out a putt? Get realistic, get a better perspective, and you'll naturally have a better sense of humor about the game. You'll have a lot better time, and your friends will also appreciate it.

During the question-and-answer period at a book signing for *Zen Golf*, a man raised his hand and asked, "I only play once or twice a month, and never have time to practice. Do you have any advice for how I can improve?" Many people in the audience chuckled at the question.

"Actually I do," I answered. "Cultivate your sense of humor."

Most golfers think that if only they played better, they'd enjoy it more. It works the other way around. If only you'd enjoy it more, you'd play better.

PART 2

How We
Get In Our Own Way

*I think the definition of insanity is hoping to get a different re-
sult by doing the same thing over and over again. We can't
solve problems by using the same kind of thinking we used
when we created them.*

—ALBERT EINSTEIN

Hope and Fear

We usually think of hope and fear as opposites. However, if we look carefully, we can see that hope and fear are two sides of the same coin. Fear arises from expectation of punishment for poor results; hope arises from attachment to rewards from good results. However much you have of one, in its shadow will be the same amount of the other. If you are afraid of missing a three-foot putt, behind that is the hope that you'll make it. The more hopeful you are of winning a tournament, the greater the fear of disappointment if you lose.

We may not be aware of the hope lingering in the background of fear, or the fear hidden behind our hope. If you look carefully at any experience, you'll see that it is necessarily the case. If there were no hope, there would be nothing to fear falling short of. If there were no fear, there would be no need to hope for the best.

All our everyday concerns can be categorized into various combinations of hope and fear. We hope for pleasure and freedom from pain; we fear pain and lack of pleasure. We hope for gain and fear loss. We hope for praise and fear criticism. We hope for a good reputation and fear a bad reputation.

As a match goes on and each putt becomes more critical to the outcome, hope and fear become more intense. Greater hope gives rise to greater fear, and vice versa. They flicker back and forth that way until they reach a crescendo of anxiety that can short-circuit our clear thinking, take us out of our routine, and create tension in our grip and stroke. Our hope and fear have caused us to get in our own way.

Recognizing the patterns of thoughts and emotions that

arise when hope and fear reinforce each other will help you step out of this cycle of self-generated anxiety. Awareness with detachment provides a bigger perspective on the situation, allowing the intensity of hope and fear to subside. You can reconnect with your unconditional confidence, commit to each putt, and accept the result without self-criticism.

Ruining a Round at Cypress Point

Cypress Point Golf Club near Pebble Beach, California, is one of the world's great golf courses. Rick and his friends had the rare privilege of being invited to play there. Rick was having a very good round, and he was relishing it. Midway through the back nine, he had a three-foot putt for par on a very challenging hole. No one said a word, and he asked, "Isn't that a gimme?" When one player said, "It's not quite inside the leather," Rick's face turned bright red with anger. He was extremely agitated at having to putt, and when he went ahead and putted, he missed badly. He remained upset for the rest of the round, and let the others in his foursome have it afterward for not giving him that putt, accusing them of being unsportsmanlike, ungenerous, mean-spirited, and the like. They looked at him as if he were a madman, and shook their heads in sadness that one putt could ruin his day at a spectacular golf course he might get to play only once in his life.

This situation demonstrates many of the obstacles that can arise in one's state of mind around the act of putting. It is a good example of how we get in our own way.

Rick was trying to avoid the pressure of a three-foot putt. What was the pressure? If he missed, he would feel as if the hard work and good shots he had made on that hole were in vain, all wasted with a blown three-footer.

He had high hopes of continuing his success that day. He had an equally great fear that missing a short putt would derail him, he'd lose his momentum, and it would be a good round turned bad. He didn't trust himself to continue to play good golf.

Most golfers have the expectation that a simple three-foot putt is missed only if they make a really poor effort, and therefore they feel embarrassed if they miss. Fear of disappointment and embarrassment adds pressure and creates anxiety.

Rick was looking for a way out of his anxiety over the putt, and transferred the responsibility for it to his playing partners. If they conceded the putt, he wouldn't have to try to hole it. His longtime habit was to finish out short putts carelessly. He felt no pressure, because he counted them as holed whether they went in or not. The problem with that habit was when a short putt was not conceded, it made the putt seem even more challenging. Avoiding pressure situations, hoping that others will give you a way out of challenging circumstances, and blaming them when things go wrong, shows a lack of mental toughness.

Rick took the refusal to concede the putt as a personal insult. He expected his fellow competitors to put his individual accomplishment of a good round above their interest in winning the match. His big-deal score was more important than their little-deal match. Being self-centered and not maintaining perspective on the situation also gets in the way of being a good partner.

Rick's pride came into play as another obstacle. As the round progressed, his mind became preoccupied with the idea of being able to say that he shot a good score on a famous golf course. That robbed him of much of the moment-to-moment delight of simply playing golf in one of the most beautiful places on earth.

Rick was also extremely competitive. He tried to get whatever advantage he could in a match. When playing with a golfer like that, the others in the foursome might well refrain from conceding a putt as a bit of payback—cutthroat competition cuts both ways. It's okay to be competitive, but be ready to take it as well as dish it out.

Other aspects of Rick's emotional makeup were revealed that day. Asking for the concession revealed his insecurity about and mistrust of his own abilities. Pouting about it for the rest of the round demonstrated his immaturity. Thinking that he was entitled to special treatment, was deprived by others of what he deserved, and that everyone had lined up against him, showed his confused perspective in relating with others.

Rick got in his own way through all these expressions of emotional reactivity and distorted thinking. He not only ruined his own round at Cypress Point, he made it a less enjoyable day for his friends as well.

This simple scenario demonstrates how putting can bring up many of the habitual patterns that create obstacles for ourselves in athletic performance and social situations. If you wisely use the opportunity that golf offers, you can learn a tremendous amount about your habits and tendencies. To get out of your own way, to free yourself from interference, you have to be an empty cup, willing to learn about yourself without preconceived ideas, and without fear of what you might find out.

Getting Ahead of Yourself

As they walked up to the tee of a long par five, Tommy asked his caddie, "Can I get home in two on this hole?"

His caddie answered, "I couldn't say. I ain't seen your drive yet."

Getting ahead of yourself means that your mind leaves the present and visits possibilities in the future. In your mind, you're thinking about making a birdie before the ball ever lands on the green.

Did you know that you can't make a birdie from the fairway? You can make an eagle if you hole out, or you can leave yourself a putt for a chance to make a birdie from the green. But thinking about making a birdie from the fairway interferes with your process of executing the shot you're playing.

In putting, thinking about the future interferes with the process taking place in the present. If you are worried about whether or not the ball will end up in the hole, you're getting ahead of yourself. How the putt finishes is something you can't control. What you can control is how the putt starts. To start the putt well, you need to focus on your process: choosing the best path you can, getting a feel for the best pace you can, going through your routine, and sending the ball rolling on its way with as good a stroke as you can. Worrying about the future only gets in the way of you making your best stroke in the present.

Thinking about how the shot will turn out before you execute it is putting the cart before the horse. Pay attention to taking care of your process, and the results will take care of themselves.

Swing, Don't Swing

Sean called me to review one of his tournament rounds. He said he'd played great from tee to green, but left most of his putts short. I asked him how freely he felt he was swinging the putter. He said, "Doc, the greens were a little bumpy. I didn't want to have a three- or four-footer coming back that might get bumped off line and end up as a three-putt. I wanted to get it there, but I kept holding back."

That gave me the answer to his problem. He was giving himself two contradictory commands: "Give it a lot of pace" and "Don't give it a lot of pace." The message his body got was to try to swing and not swing at the same time. Swing, don't swing.

Whenever you try to move forward with hope and hold back out of fear at the same time, you feel caught in the middle, very confused, not knowing what to do next. In putting, either you freeze and have a hard time taking it back, or you impulsively jab at the ball, or you combine going ahead and holding back into a tentative, decelerating stroke. None of those are likely to produce a very good result.

If you are thinking about the putt in terms of what you intend to avoid and you fear the outcome, your body will interpret that as the message, "Don't do it. You can't risk a three-putt." Intuitively you know that the only way to completely assure avoiding a three-putt is not to swing at the ball for the first putt. Yet there you are, addressing the ball, intending to putt. You are giving your body conflicting messages. Putt, don't putt. Swing the putter, don't swing the putter. You feel confused and stuck. With that state of mind, a poor putt is almost guaranteed.

PRACTICE EXERCISE:

Here's an exercise that conveys the feeling of trying to respond to contradictory directions at the same time. Try this yourself so you get a feel for the way that giving yourself mixed messages can affect you.

Hold a pen or pencil horizontally over a table, about a foot above the surface. I'm going to give you two instructions and I want you to do both of them at the same time. Wait until you have read and understood both of them. When you read the word *GO*, carry out both instructions at the same time. Be sure to do your best to do them simultaneously, not one after the other.

Instruction Number One: *Drop it.*
Instruction Number Two: *Don't drop it.*
Ready?

GO!

What did you do? If you dropped it, you did only the first instruction and not the second. If you held on to it, you did only the second and not the first.

Doesn't this feel impossible? Of course it does, because it is. Did you feel confused? That would be appropriate, because it doesn't make logical sense. How did your body feel—at ease and relaxed? I doubt it, because whatever you did or didn't do, you were wrong. Perhaps you felt stuck. That would make sense, because you were stuck between two opposing commands.

If it feels as if you're headed into that situation as you approach a putt, step back and rethink what's going on. Make a commitment to the size of stroke you intend by pre-accepting the risk of a tough comebacker. Or choose to reduce the risk by committing to a smaller stroke and pre-accepting the possibility of leaving the putt short. Pre-acceptance of a range of possible results takes the fear out of the situation. Whichever plan you commit to, you'll free yourself up to have one message, the instruction to make the stroke you intend. That way your body will have a clear image and be able to do what you ask it to. Make a plan, commit to it, then swing the putter. Period.

If I Didn't Really Try, I Didn't Really Fail

Joe really didn't like ending his round by missing a short putt, so when that prospect presented itself it brought with it a great deal of anxiety. If he had a three-footer left on the last hole, he would never mark the ball. Instead, he'd walk up and take a casual swipe at it. If he holed it, it counted. If the ball missed, he counted it anyway—rationalizing that he would have made it if he'd really tried. He soon began to do this whenever he had a short putt to save par. Before long he did it for every short putt. Joe had gotten into a bad habit.

As human beings, we seek to reduce anxiety as quickly as possible. The thought of standing around waiting for everyone else in the foursome to putt out before attempting our three-foot putt can be extremely anxiety producing. The anxiety level increases when the putt has something riding on it, such as the hole or the match. Wanting to escape the feeling of anxiety can override our desire for success. It's not a conscious choice, but our nervous system puts a higher priority on getting it over with than on getting a good outcome.

If we go ahead and putt out instead of marking the ball, it may or may not help us make the putt, but it will certainly accomplish something we unconsciously regard as more important. It will free us from the anxiety of waiting to see whether we holed it or not.

The fear of embarrassment if we miss a short putt creates anxiety. We rush to escape the anxiety, which causes us to miss the short putt. No wonder we can feel tied up in knots on the green.

Another deep-seated motivation is to protect our ego, to maintain our self-esteem in the face of disappointment. We don't do so consciously, but those feelings are likely to arise when we miss a short putt. That's why it is not such a good idea to link our feelings of self-worth to the results of a putt.

Any opportunity to remove anxiety while preserving our self-esteem becomes a pretty attractive proposition. We will go to great lengths and use elaborate logics to somehow get out of high-anxiety circumstances and protect our ego at the same time.

One way Joe protected his ego was to putt carelessly, rationalizing that he was just "getting it out of the way." Another tactic for escaping anxiety is to "give ourselves" the putt, picking it up and counting it as holed. If a playing partner complains, we say that we thought it was given. Then we set the ball back down and putt it out. If we miss, we can blame the confusion. In both of these examples we escape the anxiety of waiting to putt and at the same time have the protection that if we miss, it was because we weren't really trying. If we didn't really try, we didn't really fail.

The habit of "not really trying" so that we don't feel like we failed goes beyond putting and beyond golf. Not studying for an exam, not preparing for a meeting, procrastinating until there is too little time to do a project thoroughly, or missing a deadline for an application or audition are some of the ways we avoid the anxiety of being tested and judged. They bring with them protection from a direct hit on our self-esteem.

One of my students was genuinely distraught at the thought of preparing for a club championship. Thinking about taking lessons, working out, getting mental game coaching, and practicing as hard as he could, his concern was summed up in one poignant question: "What if I give it my all and still don't win?" The implications of failure went beyond that one tournament. It even went beyond meaning that his game wasn't good enough. He saw it as meaning that *he* wasn't good enough. Because he was tying his self-esteem to the results of a golf tournament, not winning meant that he wasn't a worthwhile person. When we choose not to play rather than risk defeat, it means we're not *playing* golf, we're *working* golf. Pure play, just having fun, has no concern for success or failure. Work, striving, and struggling do. If we're using our golf score as the measure of our value as a human being, that's a lot of work, and can't be much fun.

Not giving it our all provides us with a built-in excuse for failure. If we win, that's great. We can even brag about winning without our A-game. But if we lose, we have an out. We didn't really show up with our best. Another way to save face is to have an excuse for anything that goes wrong. Blame is often the basis of ego-protecting excuses. Either someone or something prevented us from doing our best. People were waiting in the fairway. I didn't want to step in his line. Someone was moving in my backswing. The alarm clock didn't go off. My caddie talked too much. My coach told me the wrong things to think about. It was too hot. It was too cold. It rained. They didn't fix their divot. They didn't rake the bunker. The creative possibilities for blame and excuses are endless.

The remedy is to develop mental toughness by going directly against the grain of the habit. I asked Joe to make a point of marking *every* three-footer. He was to always allow another player to go first, so that Joe would be the last one to putt out, often with people waiting impatiently in the fairway. He was to always do his full routine, settle into his address, and putt.

At the same time, I asked him to devote some time to building conditional confidence by practicing short putts. He was to hole eighteen in a row from three feet every day. Then he could confidently feel that he could play a full round and not miss one.

Joe was very intent on changing his habit. He waited to putt out whenever the situation arose. He spent enough time on the putting green at the course (and on the carpet at home) to feel quite comfortable and confident over a short putt. Before long, his anxiety was replaced with the feeling of looking forward to the challenge, and he became regarded as a player who "never misses those short ones." Ironically, the very putts that had caused him so much anxiety were now ones that his opponents regularly began to concede.

Action Reaction

Watching players practice, you can see it. They miss the first putt on the left side, then they miss the next putt on the right side. All they really accomplished was a good job of not missing it left. They didn't do such a good job of holing the putt.

The same thing happens when you miss a putt on the low side; you overcompensate on how you read the next putt and miss on the high side. A tour pro told me that he thought half the shots his fellow golfers play are reactions to one of their own or to one of their fellow competitors' previous shots.

During a tournament, one of the players I coach took more time than usual on a short putt. He was overthinking and overreading the putt, and he missed it. The next time he faced a short putt he rushed everything in his routine. He missed that putt as well. In our review of the round, we agreed that he had overcompensated for overthinking by hurrying the second putt. He did a poor job of executing his shot independent of previous experience.

I am not suggesting that you try to ignore a poor shot. The point is to consciously choose how you *respond* to it instead of unconsciously *reacting* to it.

The remedy to the problem of reaction and compensation is to fully process any unsatisfactory effort during your post-shot routine so that it doesn't carry over and inappropriately influence your next shot. You want to learn from what happened and then let it go.

Clear any emotional reaction and objectively observe what happened. Take a moment to reenact the process in the way

that you would have preferred to do it. Consider the reenact-
ment to have addressed the issue, so that you do not have to
compensate for your past mistake the next time you face a similar putt.

You can use a mental image of tearing a used sheet of paper
off a pad, leaving a clean sheet for the next plan. Your mind is
clear and you can commit to your routine on the next putt.

Rather than get caught in the cycle of compensation and
overcompensation, learn from what you observed, program a
better swing, and clear the memory banks. Then you can play
the next shot with a fresh start, not as a reaction to the last one.

Watch Your Language

One day I ran into my friend Ken and asked him how his Sat-
urday game had gone. He said that when he got home after the
round, he reflected on it and thought, "If that's the way I'm going to putt, I might as well just wake up in the morning, look in
the mirror, scream 'You idiot!' thirty-five times, and save myself a whole lot of time and money."

Calling yourself negative names does more harm than
good. If someone insults you, it hurts. Although you may not
realize it, it doesn't feel good to hear an insult coming from the
person who knows you best—yourself. It affects you even if you
think you're just saying those things in a joking or self-effacing
way. It subconsciously moves you toward believing that you actually have those negative qualities or lack of ability, and undermines your confidence.

The language that we use affects our behavior more than

we realize. That's because we not only say what we say, we also *hear* what we say. What we hear affects what we think, how we feel, and how we act. What we say about ourselves has the most powerful impact on our state of mind, because our own opinion holds more weight than anyone else's opinion about us.

If I were to point out someone walking up to the first tee and say, "That guy stinks at golf," what kind of tee shot would you expect from him? Not a very good one, I'm sure. In the same way, if you say something negative about your putting, what kind of putt are you going to expect from yourself? Out of that negative expectation, fear of a bad result arises and you tense up. You make a protecting, guiding, defensive stroke that produces exactly what you expected—a poor putt. Your opinion is confirmed, you proclaim your self-criticism for all to hear, and you dig yourself deeper into the cycle of negativity. Not a lot of fun.

The best thing you can do is to change your language habits. Easy to say, but changing habits takes work. You can read more about the habit-changing technique of combining intention and nonjudgmental awareness in the chapter "Changing Habits" in Part 7. In this case, the first step is to establish a strong intention to use less negative language about yourself or your actions. Then on your scorecard write *negative self-talk* and just make a mark whenever you notice that you have said something negative about yourself. Do so in an objective way, not judging yourself harshly when you make such a remark. That judging is just more negativity. If you do, make another mark.

At first you need count only the times you express negative self-talk out loud. When you are doing less of that, you can include negative comments that you think to yourself. It's a good thing to gradually expand that habit change to refrain from in-

sulting others as well. It does no good to create a general environment of negativity. All you have to do is be mindfully aware
of how you feel when other people speak disparagingly about
you or your friends, and you'll know how you'd like your habits
of speech to be toward others.

Once you start refraining from negative self-talk, you can
replace it with comments that will reinforce partial successes
and give you something to build on. Instead of saying, "I pushed
that putt out to the right like an idiot," you can say, "That was
the perfect pace. If I can trust my read and commit to where I
aim, I won't push or pull my putts." That is the kind of language
that will get you headed in the right direction.

What's This One For?

Mike had lost the last two holes to his friend Bill, who had
birdied both of them. Bill's putter was really working for him.
Mike decided to give Bill something to think about as Bill lined
up a five-foot putt. "Hey, dude, this is for your third birdie in a
row. Have you ever made three birdies in a row?"

Most of you know the rest of the story—Bill made the worst
stroke he had all day.

Focusing on the implications of a putt, the consequence of
the results, usually undermines a golfer's performance in pressure situations. Thinking about what the putt is for can distract
you from your process because it makes the outcome such a big
deal. Instead of immersing yourself in your routine and trusting
yourself to do your best, your mind dwells on future possibilities. You become preoccupied with hope of a good result and

fear of a bad result. You get worried, which makes you want to be more careful. Golfers often start thinking things like, "I've got to make sure I take it back slowly, and make sure I don't move my head, and make sure I follow through down the line." All such thoughts are like trying to give yourself a lesson while you're executing the putt. When you are self-conscious about your technique, a smooth, free stroke is next to impossible.

There is a part of those thoughts, hidden to your conscious mind, that makes them even more problematic. Whenever you say to yourself, "I have to make sure I do this correctly," the unsaid second half of your thought is ". . . or else something very bad will happen." Doing it right and getting a good result is your hope; messing it up and getting a bad result is your fear. The "or else" part of the thought increases the fear, causing more interference and significantly reducing the likelihood that you'll make a good stroke and roll a good putt.

Need to, *have to*, and *make sure* are the kinds of expressions that really get in the way. "I *need to* hole this one *for* a par save." "I *have to* sink this putt *for* the match." If a putt is *for* something important, that brings along the thought that you *have to* hole it, which brings along the thought to *make sure* your technique is right and not wrong. That's a lot of baggage to carry while you're trying to make a smooth stroke with a putter.

What the putt is *for* is only a concept. The ball, grass, and hole are all that actually exist. That is the reality. Nothing more, nothing less.

As soon as you start thinking about what a putt is for, the alarms should go off. Catch yourself and change your language to reflect what the present reality is, free from future expectations. Say to yourself, "This is a ball, five feet of grass, and a

hole, and I've made plenty of five-foot putts." Then go through
your routine and roll the best putt you can.

Lower Your Standards

Tiger Woods had just holed a clutch eight-foot putt to get into
a tournament play-off that he went on to win. He finished regulation play at ten under par. A review of his putting revealed
an amazing statistic: The last time he holed a putt longer than
ten feet was on the fifteenth hole of his *second* round. He
played over two full rounds without holing a putt longer than
ten feet. And he missed a few shorter than that as well.

Most low-handicap golfers who had similar putting experiences would lose confidence in their putting. That's because
golfers have unrealistically high standards for results.

Golfers have unreasonable expectations when it comes to
putting. Television contributes to the problem. It fosters the
illusion that professional golfers hole a lot of their putts from
long distances. It seems that way because only the players in
contention are on camera, the ones who are playing their best
and holing lots of putts. On top of that, when the cameras do
switch to someone who is not on the leaderboard, it's usually to
show the player making an amazingly long and difficult putt,
recorded earlier. In fact, the average pro holes fewer than half
the putts he attempts from eight feet or more.

When a tour player has a putt of about fifteen feet that's
relatively straight, it is common for television commentators
to say, "That's a very *makeable* putt." What does it mean to say a

putt is *makeable*? Every putt is makeable, and every putt is missable. The commentators are badly misleading their audience into thinking that if it's struck properly, there's a good chance the putt will go in. That creates false expectations as to the realistic chances of holing putts. The average pro holes a fifteen-foot putt only once in five attempts.

Why are we comparing ourselves to pros in the first place? If you do a long practice putting session every day and play six days a week, then it would be a reasonable comparison. If you are not playing golf for a living, it is unlikely that you practice that much.

When we have unrealistically high expectations, missing putts we think we should hole causes us to get overly critical. We put unnecessary pressure on ourselves, start missing short putts as well, and then lose confidence in our putting altogether. Our frustration is based on mistaken thinking and, unfortunately, it is self-perpetuating.

Why should you be frustrated at missing a so-called makeable putt when the best players in the world miss them more often than they sink them? Instead, think of every putt as makeable only in terms of the quality of execution. That's what you can control. As for the results, recognize the realistic chances of holing that putt, and don't be too hard on yourself if it didn't fall.

Start getting realistic about putting percentages. Lower your standards for holing putts to reduce your frustration, and raise your standards for your quality of execution to increase the effort you put into your process. You'll replace concern with confidence, make the most out of your ability, and get the best results.

PART 3

Training Your Mind

A calm heart and self-control are necessary if one is to obtain good results. If we are not in control of ourselves but instead let our impatience or anger interfere, then our work is no longer of any value.

Keeping your attention focused, alert, ready to handle ably and intelligently any situation which may arise—this is mindfulness.

—THICH NHAT HANH, *THE MIRACLE OF MINDFULNESS*

The Middle Way

An important aspect of good putting, good golf, and how we live our lives is finding balance. It may be physical, like finding a balanced stance or posture. It may be mental, like finding a balance between intensity and relaxation. It may be strategic, like finding a balance between risk and reward in choosing a shot to play. No matter what the situation, finding balance generally works better than ending up in either of the extremes.

Zen, and Buddhism in general, is known as the Middle Way: free from extremes in body, speech, and mind, such as the extremes of a life of pure self-indulgence versus one of continuous self-denial. The Buddha taught the Middle Way to a musician who asked him how to hold his mind in meditation. He explained, "Just the way you would tune the strings of your instrument. Not too tight, not too loose, just so." In golf and in life, it's very hard to pinpoint what is "just so," but it's not hard to say when something is too far in one direction or another. We can use freedom from the extremes to find the middle.

In coaching, I often refer to a theme from the fairy tale of Goldilocks and the Three Bears. When she entered the bears' house, Goldilocks encountered three versions of everything: two extremes and one balanced between the two. Papa Bear's porridge was too hot, Mama Bear's porridge was too cold, but Baby Bear's porridge was *just right*. Papa Bear's chair was too hard, Mama Bear's chair was too soft, but Baby Bear's chair was *just right*. For every shot they choose, for every target they aim toward, for every putt they plan, I encourage golfers to find the middle way between the extremes of risk and reward. Like Goldilocks, I prefer that they choose the path that is not too risky, not too conservative, but *just right*.

In playing the game of golf, finding the *just right* balance is the key to staying within your game plan, executing consistently, and getting the most out of every opportunity. If you reflect on your experiences, you'll find that it is when you veer toward the extremes of hope and fear that you start to get in your own way. The middle way of freedom from hope and fear is the path to getting out of your own way.

Mental Muscles

A young man had begged for a long time to become a student of a famous sword master in Japan. This young man was put off time and time again, being told that someone as impatient as he for results would not learn very quickly. When he was finally accepted, he thought he would be given a sword and his training in technique would begin right away. To his disappointment, the master gave him only a walking stick and assigned him to household tasks: fetching water from the spring, stacking wood behind the barn, sweeping the flagstone path, and so on.

Every now and then the master would jump out of hiding from behind a bush or from around the corner of a building and surprise the student, smacking him on the back or leg with the flat of his sword. At first the student would be caught unaware and end up with a painful welt. The young man became more and more vigilant, and began to sense the attacks coming and fend them off with *his walking stick. Eventually no matter how suddenly the master lunged, he couldn't catch the student off guard. No matter where the blow came from, the student was ready with a defense.*

In this way he was trained without knowing it, and eventually became the greatest swordsman in the land.

Our bodies possess the inherent capacity to execute a variety of actions, but we aren't necessarily functioning at the level of strength that we could be for each one. In the same way, we all possess the faculties for the mental game skills necessary for good golf, including awareness, concentration, and discipline. We don't have to learn any new ones, in the same way that we don't have to get any new muscles when we train physically. However, just as we have to strengthen our physical muscles, we also have to strengthen our mental muscles. We can strengthen the faculties we have so that they are sharper and perform at maximum efficiency and capacity.

First we need to know what we have to work with, what our resources are. The resources we have are the qualities of our mind. Our mind possesses many qualities that are equivalent to the abilities of a well-trained gymnast. An all-around gymnast has strength, discipline, and body control; in the same way our mind can be strong and disciplined in managing thoughts and emotions. Other capabilities include coordination, flexibility, balance, quickness, precision, agility, resilience, and stamina. Training the mind begins with an honest self-assessment of our level of functioning for qualities like these. When we observe our own state of mind nonjudgmentally, insight about the way our mind works arises spontaneously.

Once we have observed our strengths and weaknesses, we can practice the techniques of mind training to enhance our level of mastery until we are thoroughly trained. To be thoroughly trained does not mean perfection. It means that we are sufficiently in tune with our state of mind to know what we are experiencing as we are experiencing it.

For example, a skilled rider's training is such that the very feeling of losing his balance in the saddle initiates the movement that brings him back into balance. Sometimes we stray into unhelpful patterns of thinking and emotional reactivity. If we are well trained, our awareness brings us back to the present moment, with a spacious openness to whatever insight arises from the journey.

Mind and Body in Harmony

The first step in training your mind is to understand its relationship to your body. Mind and body need to be synchronized. The body is always in the present, so mind training involves the practice of bringing your attention back to the present when it wanders into thoughts of the past or future. That is mindful awareness of the moment.

Practicing mindful awareness is best begun by sitting still. When we stand, there is a tendency to move; when we lie down, there is a tendency to fall asleep. We sit up when we're paying attention, as when we're so interested in something that we're on the edge of our seats.

When beginning mindful awareness practice it is also helpful to find a quiet place. Until we strengthen our concentration, the hustle and bustle around us will continually distract us. After we're well trained, we can maintain our mindful awareness while in the midst of a busy place, or under the pressure of a putt for the match.

Find a place where you can sit undisturbed for as long as you intend to practice. You can sit on a thick cushion or two with your legs crossed in front of you, or you can sit on a chair. If you're on a cushion, it should be thick enough so that your knees are lower than your hips, to reduce the strain on your back. In a chair, sit in the center without leaning against the back. Your feet can be flat on the floor, or loosely crossed in front of you to keep your knees lower than your hips.

A Proper Posture

A proper posture makes it easier to stay attentive, and easier to breathe. First, feel that the joints you sit on, where your buttocks join the backs of your legs, are sinking or pressing into the seat of the chair or cushion. Let the seat support you. Next, feel that the back of your head gently extends upward. You'll feel your spine become upright but not rigid, and your chin tuck in slightly. To get the proper feeling of this, stand with your shoulder blades against a wall, and gently bring the middle of the back of your head to the wall.

There will be a slightly taut feeling from your seat to the top of your head, as your spine is straightened by the gentle extension upward toward the top and downward into your seat. Let the rest of your body soften and relax, so that you feel as if your spine is a tent pole and the rest of your body is like cloth hanging loosely from the top of the pole.

After setting your posture this way, you can tell if you are sitting up straight by applying the balance principle presented earlier in the chapter, "The Middle Way." Tilt gently to the right, feeling what it is like to be tilted too much that way. Then do the same to the left. Gently tilt side to side in smaller amounts, until you find the place that feels not tilted to one side or the other. Next do the same process tilting forward and back. You find the center by being free from tilting in any direction: not one side or the other, not front or back, but just right.

This posture is also helpful in putting. Good putting posture has the same feeling of the spine being straight, extending up and forward from the back of your head and down and back from your tailbone. With that posture, it is easy to rotate around the axis of your spine, letting your arms swing freely beneath your torso. A curved back creates strain; proper posture supports your back when you play and practice.

To complete the proper posture for mindful awareness practice, let your upper arms hang straight down from your shoulders. Bend your arms at the elbows, placing your hands palm down on top of your thighs or palm up, one over the other, in your lap. Let your jaw muscles soften, leaving your lips lightly closed or just barely parted, whichever is more comfortable. Leave your eyes open, looking forward and slightly downward. They look in one direction, but are not focused tightly on a spot. Your gaze is soft. Without moving your eyes, your awareness is open to your full field of vision.

Simply taking this posture promotes alertness. You are sitting upright without being uptight. You are in the best position to be aware of your thoughts and perceptions. You are ready to train your mind.

Settling the Body, Centering the Mind

Having established proper posture, the next step in mind training is the process of getting settled and centered. When our bodies and minds are tense and scattered, they don't serve us very well. When we are feeling grounded and at ease, settled and centered on our seat or in our stance, we function at our best.

For settling and centering, I recommend two main techniques: (1) the body scan and (2) rhythmic breathing.

The Body Scan

You can use your awareness to mentally scan throughout your body to identify residual tension and gently dissolve it. Having taken your sitting posture, tell yourself that whatever excess tension you encounter in any area of your body will soften just by your awareness resting on it, like sunlight melting snowflakes in the morning.

Begin to scan for tension, starting from the top of your head. Scan from the top of your scalp down the back of your head, then across your facial muscles. Tension often gathers in the jaw, neck, and shoulders, so pay particular attention to those areas as your awareness touches on them. Scan your arms and hands as well. Be aware of any tension you experience throughout your torso, front and back, from shoulders to genitals. Pay particular attention to your deep belly, another place where tension tends to accumulate. Complete your scan by moving your awareness down each leg from your hips and upper thighs to your feet and toes.

In any area where substantial tension continues to be felt, use your breathing to further dissolve it. Imagine that as you breathe in and out, the air is moving through the tense muscles, softening as you breathe in and cleansing as you breathe out.

Notice the difference between the tension you are using to maintain your posture and the residual tension that you were not previously aware of. In your putting stance you want only the minimum tension required to maintain your posture and hold the putter. It is the excess tension from anxiety that interferes with making a smooth, flowing stroke.

When you practice the body scan as part of a mind training session, do it slowly and thoroughly, being fully aware of each area of your body. As you become familiar with the practice, you can do a shorter version to settle yourself between activities. To prepare for that, coordinate the body scan with your breathing. Scan a section of your body each time you breathe in and out. Scan your head and neck in one breath, both shoulders and arms in the next breath, then your torso front and back, then hips and genitals, then legs and feet. Continue to practice by doing the scan in three parts with three breaths, then two, and finally scan from head to toe in one breath.

You can use the one-breath version of the body scan on the golf course before you play a shot. It will be especially helpful when facing a pressure putt. Breathe and scan your body to dissolve excess tension before you set up for your stroke.

Rhythmic Breathing*

Rhythmic breathing has been used for centuries in classical yoga. We can use it as a settling and centering technique, mentally counting as we breathe in and as we breathe out to establish a calming rhythm. The exhalation is done a bit more slowly than the inhalation, and there is a pause as the breath is held briefly between each phase. For example, we might breathe in to a count of three, "In, two, three, and hold." Then gently breathe out to a count of four, "Out, two, three, four, and hold." The word *hold* marks the points at which you hold the in-breath in for a second or two, and leave the out-breath out for a second or two. You can start with the counting as described here, or use whatever counting pattern is comfortable for you. As you get more settled, you can change numbers to find your ideal count, or change the tempo at which you mentally say each number in the count. With experience, you can try inhaling at the same pace as you exhale.

You can also enhance this exercise with a calming or settling statement that reinforces how you'd like to feel. For example, as you breathe in you can say, "Centered, two, three, hold." As you breathe out you can say, "Settled, two, three, four, hold." Words like *at ease*, *calm*, *grounded*, *soften* are also helpful to use.

By taking your seat with proper posture, and using the body scan and rhythmic breathing to ease tension and become more settled and centered, you have established the foundation for training in mindful awareness practice.

---

*Persons with respiratory issues should consult a health professional before doing any breathing exercise.

Mindfulness
and Awareness

Mindful awareness practice begins with cultivating one-pointed attention. We want to sharpen our ability to focus and concentrate. It's common for golfers to encounter some interference when standing over a putt, from either external or internal distractions. Jack Nicklaus has stated that when he was at his best he was so focused over a putt that you could shoot a gun off by the side of his head and he wouldn't notice it. I don't know that anyone's tried, but Jack is making the point that it is possible to be completely one-pointed and focused. This is a drawing-in of the mind, concentrating to the exclusion of distraction. In the Buddhist tradition, it is called *mindfulness*. Our minds are full of the experience of the present moment, undistracted and unmoved by anything. It is sometimes referred to as *bare attention*, or *just noticing*. It means to experience each moment without adding anything to it mentally. Simply notice what appears without judging, categorizing, or commenting on it.

Mindfulness is being precisely focused on what we're doing while we're doing it. Mindfulness functions in the atmosphere of *awareness*. Our thoughts and perceptions come and go, moment by moment. Awareness is the spacious perspective within which we can be mindful of what is taking place in our continuously changing experience. Combining precision and perspective, we can be mindfully aware of our world and ourselves, constantly present and responsive to whatever arises.

We can choose to emphasize either focused mindfulness

or panoramic awareness at different points in our activities. In putting, we start by taking a big perspective, looking at the lay of the land, the overall slope of the green, and an awareness of the general area that will include the path of the putt from the ball to the hole. Then we want to shift to a more precise picture of how we expect the ball to enter the hole and the pace at which it needs to be rolling. We want to be fully present and focused so that we can execute our putting routine free from distractions.

If we're always in the present, how do we learn from the past or plan for the future? Within the context of mind training, when we have a need to think about something in the past or the future, we're *awake* to the fact that we are thinking about the past or future within the space of present awareness. In other words, we can have thoughts of the past or future knowing that they are just thoughts, and not be taken away by them.

That's how we work with the relationship of mindfulness and awareness. We're noticing when we're off in daydreams and when we're back in wakefulness. We have some perspective on our situation, a big mind approach. We can be mindful of our thoughts and know them for what they are.

Structuring Your Mind Training Session

Every mind training session begins with taking one's seat with proper posture, followed by spending a little time getting settled and centered. From that ground we begin the four stages of mindful awareness practice: mindfulness of sense perceptions, mindfulness of breathing, mindful awareness of breath and space, and panoramic awareness.*

PRACTICE EXERCISE 1: Mindfulness of Sense Perceptions

We use mindfulness to connect to the present moment by shifting our focus from one particular sense perception to another—the sense of sight, the sense of sound, and bodily sensation or feeling. You can also focus on taste and smell, but we don't use those all that much on the golf course. Just notice as much as you can, without adding mental commentary, as you focus on different aspects of what you perceive. This is *mindfulness of sense perceptions*.

With eyes open, soften your gaze to expand your peripheral vision. Let visual details fill your awareness, moving around your visual field from one item to the next by shifting your attention while leaving your eyes looking straight ahead. Then, with eyes still open, turn your attention to sounds near and far, and in all directions. Notice how sound becomes more prominent, and you hear things you didn't hear when focusing on vision. Finally, still keeping your eyes open, turn your attention to bodily sensations—your weight on the

---

*My two main meditation teachers were the Tibetan master Chögyam Trungpa and his principal student, Ösel Tendzin. The basic practice of mind training they taught was a combination of mindfulness and awareness. Although the practices described in this book are sufficient for application to golf and everyday experiences, if you wish to delve deeper into the mindful awareness practice in the Buddhist tradition, it is important to have personal instruction from a qualified teacher. For information about resources for instruction, please e-mail: Info@ZenGolf.com.

chair, feet on the floor, head balanced on your neck. Feel your clothes on your body and the air on the skin of your face and hands. Feel your torso moving subtly as you breathe in and out. Because sense perceptions occur only in the present, through this practice you can experience being in the present moment with bare attention for longer than you might have thought possible.

PRACTICE EXERCISE 2: Mindfulness of Breathing

We practiced mindfulness of sense perceptions to connect to the present moment. Although it is our intention to remain present, there is a habitual tendency for our minds to wander. Sights and sounds and even bodily sensations change over time. One constant in our experience is our breathing. When our minds wander off in thoughts, we know that we have something dependable to return our attention to in the present. We return to our breathing.

In this practice you count your breaths as they go in and out, without consciously directing or manipulating your breathing in any way. This technique has been taught for over 2,500 years with these simple instructions: "When breathing out, notice that you're breathing out. When breathing in, notice that you're breathing in. If it is a short breath or a long breath, notice that it is a short or long breath." This is *mindfulness of breathing*.

In a very focused way, completely tune in to the details of your breathing. Count each breath as you experience it in the present moment. Be mindful of what it feels like for the breath to come in through the nostrils and go down into your body, then come back up and go out into the space in front of you. Notice how your body feels when the breath is filling it and how it feels when the breath goes out. Just notice your experience, without mental commentary about it.

The practice of mindfulness of breathing includes training in returning to the present moment. If you lose track of the count, bring yourself back to counting the breaths at the last number you remember. If your mind wanders, when you realize it has, simply return your focus to the breathing and counting process, without comment or judgment.

PRACTICE EXERCISE 3: Mindful Awareness of Breath and Space

Having practiced settling and centering, and having cultivated a focused mindfulness, the next component of training the mind is to develop a more expanded sense of awareness. We turn our attention to the breath moving out into the space of the room. Then we just rest in that space as our breath comes in, without needing to pay particular attention to it. We continue the practice of opening out and resting in spaciousness again and again as the basis for developing greater awareness. In that spaciousness, we can begin to work more directly with our thought process. Our minds are slowed down through relaxation training and focused through mindfulness practice. Within *mindful awareness of breath and space*, we can experience thoughts and sense perceptions arising clearly and distinctly.

We begin to notice the difference between being awake and daydreaming. When our minds are in the past or the future or wandering off somewhere else in the present, we're really not awake to the direct experience of the present moment. We're asleep in some sense to the here and now. The ideal state of mind is to be as awake and continuously present as we can be.

The practice of working with thoughts and emotions in mind training involves the technique of *labeling and returning*. When you realize that your mind has wandered into the past or the future, or elsewhere in the present, simply make a mental note, labeling it as "wandering." Do so very matter-of-factly, without judgment or guilt. Then return to the cycle of breathing and reconnect with the process of opening out into spacious awareness. Don't get discouraged if you find yourself wandering quite a bit. You can't force yourself to stay in the present. Continue the practice of labeling and returning, and eventually your mind will settle down by itself, like a dog that's gotten tired of chasing its own tail.

PRACTICE EXERCISE 4: Panoramic Awareness

The final stage of a mind training session is to expand your *panoramic awareness* infinitely in all directions. It is an extension of the mindful awareness practice we just discussed. The intention is to gradually expand the scope of what your awareness includes. With a very soft gaze, looking straight ahead at eye level, imagine that your awareness is extending in all directions. Start with the room you are in and gradually expand farther and farther, being open in all directions to the surrounding area, to the horizon, beyond the horizon to the sky, beyond the sky into space, and beyond the farthest star you can imagine. It is not that your awareness goes out in one or another direction at a time;

rather, it is truly panoramic and open to all directions at once. Rest for a minute or two in that vast spaciousness.

In that state you are completely open and your mind is limitless. You are as open and expansive as you can be. Paradoxically, you are also as centered as you can be. That is the state of mind that is the ideal foundation for everything you think, say, or do.

Summary of a Mind Training Session

- Establish your seat and proper posture.
- Use the body scan and rhythmic breathing to get settled and centered.
- Explore your sense perceptions to connect with the present moment.
- Count your breaths for one-pointed attention.
- Mix breath and space for mindful awareness.
- Expand into space in all directions for panoramic awareness.

Start every session with a few minutes on posture, settling, and sense perceptions. For beginners, spend most of the rest of your session on counting breaths, ending with a few minutes on mixing breath and space and on expansive awareness. After you have some experience, begin the same way but spend only a few minutes on counting breaths. Spend most of your time on mixing breath and space, and finish with a minute or two on expansive awareness.

Beginners can start doing sessions that are ten minutes long. As you get more accustomed to doing the practices, you can gradually make your sessions longer until they are as long as forty-five minutes, like a good physical conditioning session. The amount of time is up to you. Rather than go on until you are too tired to concentrate, end your session while you are still fresh and inquisitive, and resume again later.

Mindful Awareness in Action

Zen students are apprentices for many years before they begin to teach others. One monk who had recently become a teacher was traveling through the countryside. He stopped at the monastery of a master with whom he had studied years before. He was looking forward to having the master see how far he had come in his practice, and that he was now himself a teacher.

It was monsoon season, and he wore rain shoes and carried an umbrella. He left them in the vestibule and came into the sitting room to meet the master. After exchanging greetings, the master asked, "Out in the vestibule, did you leave your umbrella on the right or left side of your rain shoes?"

Not being aware of how he had left his belongings, the new teacher realized he had further to go in cultivating his practice of mindful awareness.

Mindful awareness in action means simply noticing the activity you're doing while you're doing it. You can practice it by observing yourself perform a simple activity such as drinking from a glass of water.

Start by sitting in good posture, in a chair facing a table with a glass of water on it. Establish the intention to mindfully reach out and pick up the glass, bring it to your lips, take a sip of water, set it down again, and put your hands back in your lap. Do the whole process in extremely slow motion, so that you can observe subtle details of your actions that you likely have never noticed before. Practice just noticing with bare attention, not adding commentary or judgment.

When you have completed the process, rest for a few moments, simply being aware of your body and your breathing.

Next, repeat the sequence of actions going a little bit faster. Move slowly enough that you are aware of and notice most of the details. Continue to repeat the process, increasing your pace of movement until you're moving at as close to a normal pace for that activity as you can without losing mindfulness of movements as you are doing them.

You may discover that when you move mindfully, just slightly slower than usual, you're moving very gracefully. You maintain your posture, you move your hand, and you take your drink in a very elegant way. This mindfulness of movements is precisely the training used in various martial arts of Japan. In performing calligraphy, in performing tea ceremony, and in performing *orioki*, the ritual serving and eating of food, one moves mindfully and gracefully. My teacher described it as the expression of art in everyday life.

Practice mindful awareness in as many other simple daily activities as you can. Brushing your teeth, making your bed, getting dressed, opening and walking through a door, picking up a pen and writing, setting the table, doing the dishes, sweeping the floor—any such simple, daily activity is a great opportunity to practice mindful awareness. Drinking and eating mindfully is also good for your health and well-being.

When it comes to golf, mindful awareness in action was intuitively practiced by the great champion Ben Hogan the

morning before any tournament round. Hogan would intentionally move in slow motion. In essence, he was doing everything in a simple, mindful way. He felt that moving in that way
set the ideal tempo for his routine in playing every golf shot
that day. In the same way, we can practice everything we are
doing mindfully: taking out our clubs, putting on our shoes,
stretching, and going through our warm-up routine.

It's very important to note the difference between mindful action and self-consciousness. It is not helpful to self-
consciously watch what you're doing with a critical eye, directing
yourself while you're doing it, and bringing to it a sense of
judgment and worry about how well you're doing it. In mindful
awareness, you're being an objective observer, simply noticing
how you're moving through any action, without any judgment
about the quality or results. Mindful awareness in action
is an opportunity for discovery and exploration, uncovering
subtleties that you didn't know about. Self-consciousness is
trying to do things in a particular way, trying to make them
come out right, and worrying about whether or not you're
succeeding.

Ideally, we want to be mindful of the process of making a
putt or any golf swing. We want to be present, aware of what
we're doing while we're doing it, without self-consciously looking over our own shoulder. When we apply mindful awareness
to our golf game, we can recognize our patterns, reinforce the
successful ones, and learn from our mistakes. We can train our
mind to be a great vehicle as we travel the path of continual improvement.

Don't Let Your Mind Take the Shape of Your Thoughts

The great Tibetan teacher Milarepa instructed one of his students to rest in awareness, experiencing the quality of her mind to be like the sky and like the ocean. She practiced for some time and then returned. She said, "I practiced as you said, but got disturbed by clouds of emotions in the sky of my mind, and waves of thoughts in the ocean of my mind."

He replied, "See the clouds of emotions as the play of the sky of your mind. See the waves of thoughts as the play of the ocean of your mind. The clouds come and go without affecting the nature of the sky. The waves rise and fall without affecting the nature of the ocean."

One of my teacher's instructions to people who became overwhelmed with a particular problem was, "Don't let your mind take the shape of the situation. Don't let your mind take the shape of your thoughts."

We get caught up in our thoughts in the same way we get wrapped up in a movie. At first we know that it's a movie. But when we get fascinated by the images and characters and plot, we get drawn into it, reacting as if it's real. When we realize we are an observer rather than a participant in the movie, our experience of it changes immediately.

To observe anything, we have to have space between ourselves and what we're observing. We can't see anything that is too close to our eyes. To create the space within which we can

relate to our thoughts and emotions, we employ mindful awareness practice. Using our breathing as an anchor to the present,
we can sit still and observe what arises moment to moment in
our mind: thoughts, emotions, and perceptions that come and
go in a seemingly continuous stream.

In the Buddhist understanding of mind, thoughts are considered to be objects of sense perception, along with sights,
sounds, smells, tastes, and bodily sensations. These latter five
senses receive input through the sense organs: eye, ear, nose,
tongue, and body. The eyes are the receivers of light, the ears
are the receivers of sound, and so on. Mind is not a sense or-
gan, yet it is a receiver. What it receives is thought. Although
you can't smell your nose or taste your tongue, your mind can
"hear" its own thoughts. A thought generated by your own mind
during your backswing can distract you even more than the
sound of someone else talking.

How can we free ourselves from the distractions of our own
thoughts? The insight leading to that freedom comes from asking another question: "Who or what is watching our thoughts?"
If our mind is observing our thoughts, there must be an aspect
of our mind that is containing the thoughts. There must be a
quality of mind itself that is different from thought.

That quality of mind can be discovered only by direct ex-
amination through the techniques of mindful awareness.
When we look closely, we find that the nature of mind is pure,
content-free awareness. Mind is like a clear glass jar that can
be filled, emptied, and refilled again and again with a variety of
different colors and textures of food and drink. In the same
way, mind is clear awareness that takes as its objects the myriad
thoughts and emotions that continuously emerge and subside.

The more we practice mindful awareness, recognizing the
nature of our mind and what arises in it, the better we are able

to identify with the container rather than the contents. Identifying with the awareness that observes the thoughts rather than with the thoughts themselves provides the spaciousness to respond with perspective rather than react compulsively with the urgency our thoughts often seem to demand. That is what is meant by not letting your mind take the shape of your thoughts.

When we're on the putting green, on the golf course, or anywhere else, we can become caught up in our thoughts: hopes and fears about the results of the round, opinions about our fellow competitors, speculations of what other people think of us, and so on. If we let our mind take the shape of these thoughts, we lose track of what's actually happening, mistaken ideas take over, and our emotional reactions get in our own way.

Through mindful awareness practice, you can deepen and stabilize the realization that your mind is more than your thoughts. Then you can continuously return to the awareness that encompasses all of these thoughts, and can make more realistic and more successful choices in playing your game and relating with others.

PRACTICE EXERCISE:

Here is an exercise that gives you a taste of the freedom that comes with not letting your mind take the shape of your thoughts. In a seated position, take a good posture, and establish the intention to remain there for the next few minutes. Turn your awareness to your breathing, and feel more and more settled as your breath goes in and out. Then generate this thought: "I'm thirsty so I'll get up and get a glass of water."

Don't get up. Notice the thought being there in your mind, but don't do anything about it.

If you didn't get up, then you experienced what it means to be the container of the thought instead of being caught up in it. You had enough perspective on your thought to make a choice about whether to act on it or not. The power to choose your response rather than react out of habit is an expression of real freedom.

Sandwich of the Day

My teacher recommended that we make each day a mindful awareness sandwich. Our activities are different every day. Consistency in how we relate to our experiences comes from starting each day with intention and ending with recollection. What we do is sandwiched in between.

The first thing in the morning, before you do anything else, sit quietly and establish your basic intentions for the day.

Start the day with three intentions, corresponding to body, speech, and mind.

First, establish the intention to be as mindful of your body as possible. Aspire to trust in your intuition and your abilities rather than trying too hard or outthinking yourself. On the golf course, this means swinging freely and seeing what happens, rather than manipulating your swing and steering your putts all the way around the course.

Second, establish the intention to be as mindful of your speech as possible. Aspire to refrain from negative self-talk, using positive, reinforcing language. On the golf course, practice this as part of your post-shot routine.

Finally, establish the intention to be as mindful of your state of mind as you can, coming back to the present moment when you wander into daydreams of past and future. The more present you are, the better your golf will be.

At the close of the day, before going to bed, take a few moments to reflect on the day, reviewing in a nonjudgmental way how well you fulfilled your intentions with respect to body, speech, and mind. It's not a contest; you don't win or lose. Just recollect what happened, without praise or blame. To whatever extent you were not mindful, think that tomorrow you'll do your best to be more tuned in. Reflect on what you learned from your experiences.

Having completed the sandwich of the day, sleep well.

PART 4

How to
Make Every Putt

When asked how he felt about missing a putt on the last hole
of a tournament, a veteran pro said, "I didn't miss the putt. I
made the putt. The ball missed the hole." That's exactly the
point: Let's recognize the difference between making a putt
and holing a putt. . . . You may not hole every putt, but you
can make every putt.

—ZEN GOLF: MASTERING THE MENTAL GAME

Putting Is a Relay Race

When I ask golfers their definition of making a putt, the nearly unanimous response is, "The ball going in the hole." I explain that it's more helpful to have a different definition for *making* a putt, one that focuses on process rather than result. If you rolled the ball on the path you chose, at the pace you wanted, with what you felt was a good stroke, then you *made* the putt. The ball going in the hole is the definition of *holing* a putt. You may not *hole* every putt, but you can *make* every putt.

We can roll the perfect putt, but we may not hole it because the green is an imperfect surface. If our confidence depends on how often the ball falls in the hole, we are in trouble. It is far better to focus on how well we execute what we intend rather than on how it turns out. That allows us to base our confidence on something we can control rather than on something that is beyond our control. Success is determined by the quality of execution, independent of the outcome.

Masters and PGA champion Jackie Burke, Jr., used two equations to represent the relationship between process (P) and results (R). He said that P over R = \$, and R over P = zero. In other words, emphasizing results over process gets you nowhere, but when you emphasize process over results, you hit pay dirt. That relationship between process and results is the foundation for the ideal attitude in *Zen Putting*. You can make every putt when you define making the putt as successfully completing your process and letting the results take care of themselves.

The key aspects of quality of execution in putting are roll, path, and pace. Making a good stroke, one that sends the ball with an end-over-end roll, is one part of successful execution. If the ball starts out traveling on the path you intended, that's another part of successful execution. If the ball starts out moving at the pace you intended, that's the third part of successful execution. That's all you have control over. Once the ball is on its way, you've done your job. Now it's the ball's job to find the hole.

Accomplishing your plan for those three components defines *making* the putt. You know after the ball has rolled just a foot or two whether you made a good stroke and started the ball on the path you intended at the pace you intended. If you did, you made your putt, whether or not you holed it.

Putting is a relay race. In a relay race, all you can do is run your section the best you can, and then make as good a handoff of the baton as you can to the next runner. After that, you just join in the cheering. In putting, swinging the putter is like running your section of the race. Transferring energy through the putter to the ball with the best direction and pace you can is like making a good handoff of the baton. Then watch the ball go on its way and root for it.

Sending It Along

In the relay race of putting, the handoff of the baton is the quality of contact by which the putter head transfers energy to the ball. There are important differences between *hitting* at the ball with the putter head versus *sending* the ball along the path with a good swing. The feel we want of stroking the putt is soft and smooth. The idea of hitting the ball is hard and quick. If you're hitting at the ball, the ball becomes the target. If you're sending the ball along the path, the target is at the end of the path. If the ball is the target, there is a tendency to stop all the action at the ball. If the target is at the end of the path, the swinging movement sweeps through the ball and continues in that direction. Thinking of sending the ball along the path rather than hitting at the ball helps you connect with the target and frees you from being ball-bound.

During a golf tournament broadcast, the commentators were complimenting David Toms's putting technique, saying, "There's one of the few players whose putting stroke really looks like his practice stroke, like he's swinging the putter without a ball there. The putter just swings and the ball happens to be in the way." That's a great description of what it means to send the ball along the path.

> *The putting stroke is not intended to be an act of hitting at the ball, but rather a feeling of sweeping it along the green. It's as if you're swinging a little broom with soft bristles instead of striking a nail with a hammer.*
>
> —BOBBY JONES

Putting to Nowhere

Ben Crenshaw, one of the all-time great putters, was doing a putting clinic and told the audience that he always made his best stroke when he wasn't putting at a hole. Peter Jacobsen, the Tour's designated comedian, chimed in, "There you have it, folks: Ben Crenshaw's secret to great putting. Don't putt at the hole!"

Funny as that sounds, it turns out to be true. Anytime you putt toward a hole, relating to distance and direction invites the tendency to manipulate the path and tempo of your swing. To get a true feel for your putting stroke, you need to be free of the interference arising from concerns about direction and pace. That means putting to nowhere.

Before you roll your first putt, get a feel for swinging the putter with good tempo. Take your stance without a ball, and just let the putter head swing back and forth in an easy, pendulum motion. Be mindful of your grip pressure, and do your best to keep it consistent throughout each stroke. Notice the path that the putter head takes as it passes across the grass directly under your eyes. Let your body subtly find the way to swing on a path that is perpendicular to the putter face.

After getting the feel of a fluid, rhythmic swing with no ball, you can begin putting to nowhere. Set a few balls in a row on a relatively level area of the practice green. Get comfortable in your setup, aimed toward an area of the green where there is no hole. You are truly putting to nowhere. Make a stroke that is not too big and not too small, whatever your intuition creates without conscious intention. At first, just notice the tempo of swinging, keeping your head and body as steady as when you were swinging the putter without a ball there. There is no rush to look up to see how the putt turns out—there's no hole.

Keep putting to nowhere until you feel your stroke to be one of ease and flow, making consistently solid contact with the ball that rolls end over end across the green.

Next, intentionally make the stroke smaller, so that the ball rolls only about six feet. Shorter putts are ones that make us want to guide the putter rather than letting it swing. On these putts our grip pressure typically tightens, and our hands get overly involved, pushing or pulling the ball toward the hole. Practice these short putts to nowhere until the stroke feels as flowing and natural as the longer strokes do.

Finally, alternate long, medium, and short strokes a few times, until you can maintain the same feel and tempo for all of them. Swinging the putter with your putting-to-nowhere stroke, you'll be able to better maintain your tempo and more consistently make solid, sweet spot contact. Since you're putting to nowhere, you can't miss.

PRACTICE EXERCISE: End-Over-End Roll

To find out how well you're rolling the ball, practice your putting to nowhere stroke using a ball with a line on it. Range balls often come with lines on them but you may prefer drawing a line on the brand of ball you play.

Set the ball on the green with the line across the middle of the top of the ball, and set the putter face perpendicular to that line. Then make your putting-to-nowhere stroke. If you can see the line staying sharp and stable down the middle, that means you've rolled an end-over-end putt. The putter face was square to your swing path and the line on the ball when it made contact. Any kind of glancing blow makes the line look wobbly or blurred as the ball rolls because it gives the ball sidespin rather than a purely end-over-end roll. It may be that the putter face wasn't perpendicular to the line on the ball, the putter head wasn't swinging straight along the path, or the ball wasn't struck with the sweet spot of the putter. Sidespin causes less predictable movements of the ball as it goes across the surface of the green, and therefore gives less consistent results.

If the line wobbles as the ball rolls, first check that the putter face is perpendicular to the line on the ball. Then keep making strokes, letting your intuitive mind make very subtle adjustments to find the way of swinging that produces a sharp, stable line during the roll. If you find that your most free and unguided swing still produces a wobbly line, you can check with your instructor about adjusting your stance and posture.

If the line on the ball is clear and steady, you can have confidence that when you roll a putt with your putting-to-nowhere swing, it will track straight and true down the path you send it.

Swing Bigger, Not Harder

Kenny was on the practice green at the Pebble Beach National Pro-Am, and I asked him how the tournament was going. He said he played fabulously from tee to green, but was off on his distances for longer putts all day. Short one hole, long the next. I asked if that were common for him, and he admitted that distance control wasn't the strongest part of his putting game.

Watching him roll a few putts, I noticed that on the shorter putts, his grip was gentle and he swung the putter with a fluid, even motion. On the longer putts, it appeared that he was taking the putter back about the same as he did on shorter putts, and then trying to hit the ball harder to make it go farther. To do so, he was tightening his grip on the putter as well, and I even noticed his jaw being a bit more tense.

Motioning him over, I asked him to watch me stroke three

golf balls. I asked him to notice if I were swinging faster or hitting harder at any of them. For the first ball, I let the putter head swing just a few inches back and a few inches through. For the second ball, I made a little bit bigger swing, and a bigger swing still for the third ball. The balls ended up evenly spaced, six, twelve, and eighteen feet from where they started.

The tempo was the same on all three, not faster for the longer putts. My grip pressure stayed constant, and there was no sense of a harder hit at any of them. The only difference was in the size of the swing. The swings were bigger, not harder.

He tried it, and was amazed at how easy it was. When he played to a hole farther away, he would say to himself, "Let the stroke be a little bigger." When he played to a closer hole, he would say, "Let the stroke be a little smaller." With a consistent motion, it wasn't long before he could feel subtle distinctions in the size of the swing he was making, and his distance control became excellent.

Thinking you need to hit a putt harder to make it go farther is a common misconception. In the same way that one would mistakenly think, "If I swing my driver harder, the ball will go farther," we think that for longer putts we have to make a harder stroke. That way of putting reduces your sense of feel for distance because you have to tighten your grip to move the putter head faster. It makes the roll less consistent because the sharp hitting action at the ball produces skidding and wobbling. The mental intention to hit at the ball, rather than letting the putter head swing through and send the ball along the path, takes you out of your tempo.

Trying to swing the putter differently for different distances is an unnecessary complication. And the last thing we need is to make golf more complicated. You'll find it much simpler and more effective to maintain the same tempo, grip pressure, and swing path for every putt. For different distances, the only adjustment you need to make is to let the putter head come back and through a bit longer or shorter. If this is a new technique for you, you'll need practice to see how far the ball rolls for the size of swing you make. The practice exercise "Gauging Distance by Swing Size" below will help you work on that.

For most golfers who have been taking a small stroke on long putts but just hitting the ball harder, taking a much bigger swing can be quite scary. That's because it's unfamiliar, and they fear their distance control will get worse, not better, with a bigger swing. Being afraid that a big swing will send the ball too far, they tighten up on the way through, causing the putter head to decelerate as it nears the ball.

The solution is to establish a strong intention to maintain your tempo and grip pressure for every putt. Get used to different swing sizes through practice. You'll be surprised at how big a swing you can take and not hit the ball too far when you keep your grip soft and let the putter head fall through, just the way you did when you were putting to nowhere. It will soon be more comfortable to swing bigger instead of harder.

PRACTICE EXERCISE: Gauging Distance by Swing Size

Line up five balls, about six inches apart. Start with the nearest ball and stroke a putt of about six feet. For each succeeding ball, maintain the same tempo, grip pressure, and speed of swinging the putter, while making each stroke a little bit bigger. Notice how much farther each ball goes. Then practice trying to make the putts stop at even intervals of distance. For example, try to make each ball finish three feet farther than the previous ball (resulting in putts of 6, 9, 12, 15, and 18 feet). Repeat the drill with different size intervals, such as trying to make each ball finish six feet farther than the previous ball (resulting in putts of 6, 12, 18, 24, and 30 feet). When you feel like you have a good touch for this, set ball marks at these distances and putt to the ball marks in random order to refine your feel for how big or small a stroke you need to make for each distance.

Soften Your Grip

Kevin had three-putted four times in the first round of a professional tournament. He told me that he'd just been to the putting laboratory of one of the top technical analysts in the game, and that everything looked good: stance, ball position, swing path, and all the specifications of his putter.

To look into what was happening, I asked him to start by putting to nowhere. This was to be done with only two intentions: making contact on the sweet spot and having the ball rolling nicely end over end. After several of those, we added the intention of rolling the ball different distances.

Everything about Kevin's setup looked good, but the roll wasn't all that pure, especially when he putted shorter ones. I asked him to set up to a putt and tell me when he was ready to stroke it. He said, "I'm ready," and I said, "Don't change your grip pressure. Keep it exactly as it is now. I'm going to move the putter shaft; don't change the grip pressure, no matter what I do."

Grasping the putter shaft, I tilted it away from him. "Keep the same grip pressure," I said, and started to pull the putter away from him. He was gripping it so tightly that he was pulled out of his stance rather than the putter coming out of his hands.

Then I took my stance holding the putter and had him pull it away. It slipped easily out of my hands, with just a bit of friction. I said, "Hold it as softly as I did." He stroked a couple of putts that way, and they rolled much more purely.

I had him waggle the putter with both a very soft and a very tight grip pressure. He could feel the weight of the putter head much better with the soft grip. He said that recently the putter head was sort of waving around when he took it back. Paradoxically, the tighter the grip, the more it will move around as you swing it. When the grip is tight, a slight movement with your hands will translate into a big movement at the other end of the club. He said the new grip pressure felt a little loose, and I explained that such a feeling was heightened because of the contrast between the sensation of holding the putter softly and the way he was used to holding it. I encouraged him to try out different grip pressures until he found one that felt not too tight, not too soft, but just right.

I made a point of using the word *soft* rather than *loose*. In describing the way you hold the putter, it is important to distinguish between *soft* and *loose*. Often when I suggest that golfers soften their grip, they'll respond as Kevin did, saying, "The putter feels out of control when I hold it so loosely." It is rare that something feels loose and feels in control at the same time. However, you can hold the putter softly and still feel it is in your control. In fact, you can even have a feeling of firm wrists but soft hands.

It can also be helpful to use the word *hold* rather than *grip* when describing how your hands are on the putter. *Gripping* can convey the quality of tightly grasping the putter handle. The word *holding* doesn't have any inherent feeling as to how tightly you are doing so. It's easy to say you are going to hold the putter softly; it feels somewhat contradictory to say you are going to grip the putter softly.

When you hold the putter softly and maintain that same amount of pressure throughout the stroke, it's less likely that you will guide or direct the putt. It is the same way that you putt when you're putting to nowhere. If you are mindful of your process, you'll notice that when you do alter the path of the putter head as you swing, you will have impulsively tightened your grip to do so. To maintain a soft, consistent pressure throughout his stroke, Jack Nicklaus imagined that the shaft of his putter was like the thin stem of a crystal wine glass. If his grip tightened at all before or during the stroke, the crystal stem would snap. That's a good image to give you the feel of taking and maintaining a soft hold on the putter.

Once Kevin got more comfortable with the new softer feeling, he started rolling the ball much better. At first his putts rolled farther than he expected. That made sense, since the contact was pure and the roll true. However, his softer hold gave him a better feel for the putter head. It didn't take long on the practice green for him to adjust to the new way of swinging the putter, and to start holing a lot of putts.

He'd taken thirty-five putts during his round that day. The next day he had only twenty-five.

PRACTICE EXERCISE:

Take your putting stance and hold the putter with your usual grip pressure. Tighten your hold on the putter until you are holding it as tightly as you can. Waggle the putter. You'll feel most of the weight to be in the shaft, near your hands. Soften your hold on the putter until it is as light as it can be without the putter coming out of your hands. Waggle the putter. You'll feel most of the weight to be in the putter head.

The softer the hold, the more feel you'll have of the putter head as you swing the putter, and the better feel you'll have for the pace your stroke will produce. Try putting with a range of different grip pressures to find the softest pressure you can use and still feel in control of the putter. Practice maintaining that grip pressure throughout your stroke. You'll soon develop a better feel for pace and a more consistent stroke that has the ball rolling straight down your path.

The Wrists Follow the Fingers

Through most of the twentieth century, golfers used a very "wristy" putting stroke. As the condition of greens and the design of putters improved, the ideal putting stroke became one that uses hardly any wrist action. The hands hold the putter at a constant angle and as an extension of the arms, which in turn are an extension of the shoulders and torso. The arms, hands, and putter function as one structure that the torso and the shoulders swing.

When nervousness, excitement, or other emotions influence our state of mind as we prepare to putt, it is common that the smooth flow of our putting stroke breaks down with a flipping or twisting of the wrists. When the pressure is on, our fingers tighten like a fist and transform our soft hold on the putter into a strangling grip. Softly holding the putter means the fingers aren't doing much; when they get involved in grasping the putter more tightly, the fingers become troublemakers.

The key point here is that the wrists get blamed, but it's the fingers that are causing the problems. The muscles around the wrists themselves initiate very little movement. The fingers lead the action, and the wrists follow the fingers.

Use your awareness to notice situations in which your grip pressure tightens. When you feel that happening, counter it by imagining that a feeling of softness and ease is flowing down each of your arms and into your hands and fingers, almost like a soothing liquid. If it's helpful, you can synchronize that flow of softness through your arms with a slow exhalation of your breath. Feel your fingers soften, without your hold on the putter getting too loose. Continue your routine and make a smoothly flowing stroke.

PRACTICE EXERCISE:

Hold your arms so that your elbows are at your sides and your hands are extended out in front of you, palms toward each other. Let your hands be as relaxed and limp as possible. Now try to move your wrists while leaving your fingers completely limp. Without your fingers, the wrists don't have that much range of motion. You may even find it hard to leave your fingers limp, which shows how strong a habit it is for the fingers to lead any hand movement.

Next, activate your fingers to lead the bending of your wrists in a way that extends them to the limit of your range of motion. You can see the difference when you are involving the fingers to move the wrists. It probably feels quite natural, because we typically move our hands by leading with our fingers.

When you putt, if the fingers don't get activated, if they stay very soft, it is far more likely that you will be able to leave the flipping or twisting action of the wrists out of the putting stroke. It is the fingers that activate those kinds of wrist movements and the breaking down of the stroke, not the wrists themselves. The wrists follow the fingers.

Path Versus Line

An important use of language has to do with the way we read a putt and describe the imagined route it will take as it rolls across the green to the hole. It's preferable to use the word *path* rather than *line*. A path feels nice and wide. It's easy to walk down a wide path. A line is very narrow. It's hard to walk a fine line. If someone asks you to walk down a path, you can do so without even looking. If someone tells you to walk and be sure you stay exactly on a line, you'll wobble and have to work hard to keep your balance and stay on the line. There's a reason they use walking a line as a sobriety test.

A path is more representative of the reality of how a putt travels to the hole. The hole is four and one-quarter inches wide. When traveling at a moderate pace, the ball can be rolling anywhere within a path at least three inches wide and not lip out. A ball going quite slowly as it reaches the hole can be traveling anywhere within a four-inch-wide path and still be sure to fall in the hole.

PRACTICE EXERCISE:

You can feel the difference in using the words *path* and *line*. Turn the focus of your awareness to your body. Use a settling, clearing breath to dissolve excess tension. Pay attention to how your body feels when you imagine the following two putts. First, notice the feeling when you say, "Roll it down the path," and imagine yourself doing so. Then notice the feeling when you say, "Keep it on the line," and imagine yourself putting that way. Most people feel more tension when they say the second sentence because they face a more challenging task. You'll be more settled over your putt if you know it has room to roll anywhere along the path and still go in the hole.

Connect the Dots

In some mystical golf movies, the hero miraculously sees a band of softly glowing colored light showing the path the putt will take. Sometimes it appears as a golf ball rolling in slow motion along the green and into the hole, like a vision of the future.

When golfers are told to visualize the path of a putt, they often think it should appear to them as a dramatic, movie-like experience. They think something's wrong with them if it doesn't.

In fact, few people see something so vivid. The path of a putt appears differently to everyone, and differently to each of us at different times. However you see it in your mind's eye, that's what will work for you.

Often golfers complain to me that they can't see a path when reading their putts. That was the case for Steve, one of my amateur students, who was bemoaning his lack of ability to visualize. I set a ball on a sloping area of the practice green, and pointed to a hole. "Which way is that putt going to break?" I asked.

Steve said, "Right to left." I went to a point halfway along a straight line between the ball and the hole, and put a ball marker in the ground. I reminded him that you can't choose a path without choosing a pace at which you want the putt to enter the hole, and asked, "For a putt that would trickle in at a gentle pace, does the ball need to pass to the right or left of the marker to have a chance of going in the hole?"

He answered, "To the right, obviously. It's a right to left putt."

"Good point," I said, and moved the marker an inch to the right. "How about now—inside or outside the marker?"

"Still outside. It's going to break a lot," he replied. Twice more I moved it to the right, asked again, and got the same response. The next time, he said, "Now that's too far. It would have to go just inside the marker." I moved it back and forth until he couldn't say "outside" or "inside." We had used the middle-way approach to find a point that was not too far outside, not too far inside, but just right. That meant he saw, in his mind's eye, his best guess of a point midway along the ideal path for the putt.

We then went halfway between that point and the hole, and did the same exercise until he couldn't say inside or outside again, and placed another marker there. We went through the same procedure at in-between points three more times.

The five ball markers between the ball and the hole marked points on the green that in Steve's judgment the ball would need to roll through to have the best chance to go in the hole. Steve was pleasantly surprised to realize that all he had to do was connect the markers, like connecting the dots in a puzzle, and there was his path. He had been able to see it in his mind's eye all along.

We then rolled a putt toward the first marker to see how it would turn out. The ball rolled over the first three markers. As it slowed, it turned and passed below the hole. That told Steve that he needed to see the path turning more sharply near the end as the ball slowed down. When he imagined the putt finishing that way, it was easy to see that he needed to start the putt a bit farther to the right.

Train your green reading and visualization ability by practicing in this way. Imagine the path you expect a breaking putt to take, using ball markers as points along the path if you find that helpful. Connect the dots to get a clear image of the path, and then putt along the start of that path. Watch how the ball rolls, adjust your image of the path, and then adjust your aim accordingly. Practicing in this way, you'll learn to read putts more accurately, visualize the path more vividly, and have more fun watching your ball rolling along that curving path you pictured, right into the hole.

Aim Is the Name
of the Game

One evening, a fellow was walking down a city street and saw an old man looking carefully all around the area under a street lamp. He asked the old man what he was doing. "Looking for my key," he answered, and the stranger set about helping him.

"Where exactly did you drop it?" the stranger inquired as he searched.

"Over there in the alley," the old man said.

"Then why in heaven's name are we looking over here?" he cried.

"Over here the light is much better," the old man calmly explained.

No matter how good a stroke we have or how well we read a putt, if we aren't aimed where we think we're aimed, holing the putt becomes more a matter of luck than skill. One of the most common perceptual challenges is aiming the putter face on the path we intend. It's no accident that modern putters are designed with high-tech alignment aids built in.

The problem we have in aiming the putter face toward a target happens because of the way our two eyes work together. They work best when horizontally level with each other, at equal distances from the object we are viewing, looking straight ahead. When we set up to a putt and turn our head to look down the path toward the hole, our eyes are tilted, one higher than the other, one closer to the hole than the other, looking somewhat sideways. That's why I like to say, "If we were meant to play golf, we'd be born with an eye on each side of our ear."

Because a tilted view distorts our perception, we often misjudge the direction in which we're aimed. Most people misjudge their aim in the same direction for every putt. More often than not, the putter face is aimed some amount outside (to the right for right-handers) of where we think we are aiming it.

The good news is that you can train your eyes to see differently, which is actually training your brain to interpret the images coming from your eyes differently.

A perception study done many years ago had a woman wear goggles that inverted everything in her field of vision. Everything she saw looked upside down. She felt as if she were walking on the ceiling, and when she reached to the left she saw her hand move to the right. She had to learn to move in the opposite direction of where things appeared to be to get where she wanted to go. After a couple of weeks of wearing the goggles during all her waking hours, her brain adjusted and she "saw" everything in a normal way again. The goggles still turned things upside down, but her brain reversed its usual interpretation of the visual input. She no longer had to consciously adjust her movements.

Let's take a look at factors in putting that can have an impact on your perceived aim, adjustments you can make for better alignment, and how you can train your visual perception to overcome any remaining distortion tendency.

Choose More or Less Offset on Your Putter

How much your putter face is offset from the shaft can affect your perceived alignment. Many people find that more offset counters the tendency to aim more to the outside than they think they're aimed. This differs a great deal by individual. The best thing to do is to try out a number of putters at the same time, ones with various amounts of offset from the shaft to the face. Have a friend (or a sales clerk) let you know if changes in the amount of offset, more or less, change your perception in aiming. Then choose a putter that helps minimize your perceptual distortion.

Change Your Ball Position

Sometimes ball position—near or far, forward or back—can affect how your eyes see the direction you're aiming. There is a relationship between the distance your eyes are from a point directly over the ball and the amount of your perceptual distortion. The most common pattern is a stance having the eyes too far inside of the ball, usually meaning you are standing too far away from it. From that angle, you aim farther outside the path than you intend. Standing with your eyes closer to being directly over the ball can decrease the distortion, making your perceived alignment a better match with your actual alignment.

How far forward or back in your stance the ball is positioned can also affect perception. Too far forward and you're likely to be aimed more inside than you think; too far back and you're likely to be aimed outside the path you intend the ball to travel.

Experiment with taking your stance so that the ball is different distances from you, and different distances forward or back in your stance. Ask your instructor or a friend to give you feedback on how changes in ball position affect your perception in aiming.

Use an Intermediate Target

Because a tilted view distorts your perception, sometimes the read of a putt will look one way from behind the ball and then look different when you take your stance over the ball. This creates doubt about the amount of break you've chosen to play, and undermines your commitment to the path you intend for the putt.

Find a discolored bit of grass or part of an old pitch mark on or near the path you see from behind the ball, a foot and a half from the ball. Set the putter face aimed down the path at or near that intermediate target. The challenge here is to override your perception and send the ball down the path on which you are aiming. You can say something like this to yourself: "It looks like I'm aiming at the left edge of the hole, but since my habit is to aim right of where I think I'm aimed, I know the putter face is aimed at the middle of the hole. Trust it."

Knowing that your view from behind the ball is the accurate one, even though it looks off path from your stance over the ball, make a strong commitment to trust your process of stroking the putt toward the intermediate target.

Read from Your Stance

Because the break can look different when you get into your stance, some players read the putt from their stance *first*, before looking from behind the ball. Since you'll end up there, you might try starting from there.

Train Your Perception

Set a ball about ten feet from a hole on a level spot of the green. Address the putt with the help of a friend who will tell you when your putter face is aimed straight at the middle of the hole. If you have alignment distortion, the aim will look off to you, in one direction or the other. If it seems you're aiming to the left, you have a habit of aiming right of where you think you're aimed, and vice versa.

To train your perception, put a ball marker into the ground about one and a half feet in front of the ball, as an intermediate mark on a line to the middle of the hole. From your putting stance, let your eyes slowly track from the putter face to the intermediate mark to the hole, then back to the intermediate mark and to the putter face. You may turn your head a slight bit, but don't lift your head or move your body. Track with your eyes back and forth again and again between the putter face, intermediate mark, and hole.

Do seven to ten repetitions, stand up and take a break for a minute, then do another set of reps. Take care not to do this exercise for so many sets or so often that you get eyestrain. No more than three sets at a time, no more than once an hour, no more than a few times a day. If you have any discomfort, stop immediately.*

How long it takes is a matter of individual differences, but over time many people can successfully train their eyes to see the putter as aiming in the direction they intend.

*Persons with vision issues should consult a health professional before doing any eye exercise.

Every Putt's
a Straight Putt

Of course, not every putt actually is a straight putt. The point is to swing your putter for every putt the same way you would swing it for a straight putt. Roll every putt along the start of the path you've chosen, in the direction the putter face is aiming. Then trust that gravity will move the ball in the direction you guessed it would as it rolls toward the hole.

A common fault from which even top pros suffer is the tendency to change the direction the putter head is swinging and the putter face is aiming during the stroke. They are guiding the ball as they swing the putter, pushing or pulling the putt away from the path toward which it was originally aimed.

Sometimes golfers guide the ball out away from the hole to give the putt more room to break. This is a response to a lack of trust in where the putter face is aimed, fearing that they aren't aiming far enough outside the hole. Since most golfers underestimate the amount of break in a given putt, they often find themselves aiming too much toward the hole and not far enough out along the ideal path. Subconsciously they sense that they haven't set up for enough break. As they swing, they redirect the ball farther away from the hole, either pushing or pulling it outside their original path. On the occasions that they are afraid they are playing too much break, they guide the ball as they make their stroke to pull or push it toward the hole.

Another tendency of many golfers is to be too tightly focused on the hole. Although they are aimed properly for the break they intend to play, they look only at the hole instead of letting their eyes track back and forth along the path. Since the image of the hole is the last thing in their minds, subconsciously they swing toward the hole, rather than swinging straight along the path at which the putter was aimed. The result is usually missing the putt below the hole. If that is your most common miss, but you feel you stroke straight putts, then missing low is simply the result of underestimating the break you need to play.

The remedy for pushing or pulling putts is commitment. Commit to the path you choose after reading the putt. Commit to the size of swing that will give you the pace you desire. Commit to swinging the putter the way you do for a straight putt, making your putting-to-nowhere swing that will send the ball straight along the start of the path toward which the putter face is aimed.

You'll get more consistency if you commit to your read of the path, your judgment of the pace, and your straight putt stroke for every putt.

PRACTICE EXERCISE:

If you find it challenging to commit to the path on which you're aimed, or can't tell if the ball is starting on that path, use an intermediate target in practice. Choose a medium-length putt with a good bit of break. Visualize the path on which you expect the ball to travel to the hole. Focus on the start of that path and then press down a ball mark on the path a foot or two in front of your ball. Practice the process of looking along the path and swinging the putter as if you're putting to nowhere until your putts are consistently rolling over the mark. During play you can use this technique for added confidence by picking out a little spot as an intermediate target along your path, a foot or two in front of your ball. Set up to that target, get a feel for your pace, and commit to swinging like you're putting a straight putt.

Prepare Your Process: Structuring Your Warm-up Routine

Confidence is supported by good preparation. A thorough putting warm-up routine before your round has a big influence on how prepared you feel. I recommend the following steps to all golfers, amateurs and pros alike.

Connect with Your Body

Start your warm-up routine for putting by getting in touch with how your body is feeling. You may have just gotten out of your car, or you may have hit some balls and chipped already. Before you walk onto the putting green, stand for a moment and be mindful of your breathing. Do a brief body scan, as described in the chapter "Settling the Body, Centering the Mind," in Part 3. Feel where the tension is, particularly noticing your face and eyes, your jaw, neck, shoulders, and hands, down to your abs and deep belly. These are common places where tension accumulates. Let the excess tension in all of those places dissolve—soften, relax, feel them drop into a settled position. Now you're ready to start putting to nowhere.

Putting to Nowhere

It is helpful to isolate the components of putting and sharpen them up one at a time. First your stroke, then feel for pace, then reading the path.

To warm up your stroke, get a feel for swinging the putter back and through with good tempo. The best way to do that is by putting to nowhere. Roll some putts toward an area of the green where there is no hole. Make average size swings, finding your comfortable tempo and swing path, keeping your grip soft and your head and body steady. Next, roll a few shorter and longer putts to nowhere, maintaining the same feel and tempo for all of them. Keep putting to nowhere until you feel your stroke is rhythmic and consistent, squarely hitting the sweet spot time after time.

Getting a Feel for Pace

Having warmed up your putting-to-nowhere stroke, it's time to turn your attention to feel for pace. Here are two exercises you can use.

One is like a guessing game. Set up to a putt about twenty feet from the edge of the green, where it meets the fringe. Look at the distance between the ball and the fringe, and then make what you think is the right size swing to take the ball just to the edge. The key element of this exercise is to guess, just by feel, whether you think it will end up short, long, or about right. When you look to see how it turned out, the visual feedback lets you know intuitively how much bigger or smaller a swing to make on the next one.

The other exercise uses three tees set in an open area of

the green at measured intervals. Start with the tees three paces apart, so that they are nine, eighteen, and twenty-seven feet from you. Putt to the tees in random order until you get a feel for the different swing sizes you need for those distances. Repeat the exercise with the tees two paces apart, then again with the tees one pace apart. You can also do this exercise in reverse order, from short to long putts.

If you have time in your warm-up, it's helpful to do one or both of these exercises putting uphill and downhill, as well as into and with the grain.

Getting a feel for pace is a big part of reading greens and trusting your stroke on the course.

Let the Long Putts Roll

Now that you've gotten a feel for your pace, roll longer putts, the kind that are usually described as lag putts. I don't like to use the expression "lag" putts, because it conveys the intention to roll the putt to a general area. It can lead to complacency and lack of sharpness in the process of reading, gauging feel, and routine of executing the putt. The ideal lag putt turns out to be the one that has the best chance of going in the hole, so why not play to hole every putt? This doesn't mean putting at a pace that will take the ball several feet past the hole if it misses. A putt that has the best chance stops only a foot or two past the hole if it doesn't go in.

To warm up for long putts, take your stance next to the ball and make practice strokes until you feel that the last practice stroke is the one that will produce the putt you are picturing to roll that distance. Then step into your actual stance and reproduce that feel. When you reproduce the feel of the stroke that you thought would send the ball a particular distance, you will get feedback from each putt and develop a better and better feel for the pace of long putts during warm-up, practice, and even the round.

Big Breakers

The next part of your warm-up routine is getting a feel for putts with big breaks to them. Try a variety of mid-length putts with plenty of break: left to right, right to left, uphill and downhill. Try different paths on which to play each putt until you can play for the maximum amount of break and still have the ball reach the hole. It won't be going very fast as it's getting to the hole at that point, which means if it misses the hole it won't roll too far past and leave you a tough comebacker. The idea is to test out different angles and get a feel for how pace and path work together on the greens that day. You want to find the combination with which you are most comfortable, that will encourage commitment and not give rise to doubts or second thoughts as you are addressing the ball. Keep in mind that playing for maximum break usually conserves mental energy.

Skip the Eight-Footers

What most golfers do next is practice a lot of straight, level putts of about eight feet or so. These putts are the ones you might think you need to practice most, because holing them is going to save you strokes out on the course. I completely agree that holing those putts on the course will save you strokes. Holing any putt means at least one less stroke on that hole.

However, I suggest that you do *not* include those putts as part of your warm-up routine.

There are two reasons. The first is because they are unnecessary—you don't need them to practice your feel for pace or your reading skills. The second reason is more important: You are likely to miss a lot of them. As I mentioned in Part 2, the PGA Tour average for holing eight-footers is about fifty percent. So do you want to spend your practice time missing half of what look like easily makeable putts? Do you want to implant in your memory the frustration of seemingly simple putts that don't go in the hole? Why practice missing?

Sounds of Success

Conclude your warm-up routine by rolling in several two-footers. You get the reinforcement of seeing yourself holing putt after putt. Not only do you see yourself, you also hear yourself holing putt after putt. You hear the sounds of success. Your subconscious doesn't know the difference in sound between a two-footer and a ten-footer; all it knows is that you are holing a lot of putts in a row. That's the way to build confidence. Having holed a hatful of those, now you are ready to head for the golf course.

Summary of a Warm-up Routine

- Connect with your body.
- Putt to nowhere for your stroke.
- Exercise to get a feel for your pace.
- Roll some long putts for size of swing.
- Putt some big breaking putts for feel of combining pace and path.
- Skip the eight-footers so you don't practice missing.
- Finish with two-footers for the sounds of success.

When you arrive at the course with less than your usual amount of warm-up time, you can do an abbreviated warm-up routine. Always putt to nowhere first. Then putt to the fringe to get a feel for pace, and roll a few long putts to holes. Stroke a two-footer from each of the four directions around a hole, and head for the tee.

PART 5

Putting It into Play

I never stroked a putt that I hadn't already made in my mind.

—JACK NICKLAUS

Once I've started the putter in motion, it's as if it's swinging itself.

—BEN CRENSHAW

Local Knowledge

You can get a head start on a new course before you even step on the practice green. When you are playing a course for the first time, go to the pro shop and ask for someone who plays the course often and plays it well. That person will be your source for local knowledge.

Ask about the lay of the land: Is there a general, overall direction toward which the greens on the course break? For example, in the Coachella Valley of California that is home to Palm Springs there is a local expression that "all putts break toward Indio." The whole valley slopes gradually from Palm Springs in the west to Indio in the east. All other factors being equal, putts on the valley's courses have the tendency to break a bit more in that direction than they look like they will.

Also ask if there are any greens that go against the usual pattern for the break. For example, there might be a green near a pond that is specially banked to break away from the water. Are there particular greens for which the break is much different than it appears? That often happens at courses in the mountains. Having played a lot of golf in Colorado, I've seen many a putt that I could have sworn broke uphill.

Ask if there are any other points of local knowledge that will help you in being aware of inconsistencies in the putting surfaces. On some courses there are one or two greens that get less than the optimum amount of sunlight. Often those greens can't be mown as closely, so those putting surfaces will be a bit slower than the rest.

That brings us to another important question: How closely

does the practice green resemble most of the greens on the course? Is the pace on the surface substantially slower? Do the greens on the course have more or less undulation than the practice green? How much more?

We're talking about issues related to putting, but don't let your quest for local knowledge stop there. Find out as much as you can about course conditions, hidden hazards, and other "inside information."

Getting local knowledge before you tee it up helps you be prepared for what you'll find out there. It can save you a few strokes, and can help get your round off to a much better start.

Lay of the Land

I start reading a putt when I'm still fifty yards from the green.

—JACK NICKLAUS

Wes was having some trouble reading putts, especially at tournament courses where there was an influence from elevated or low-lying areas nearby. Putts that looked level broke away from the mountains or toward the ocean. In some cases the effect was so pronounced that it created optical illusions. It looked as if putts defied gravity. Wes was puzzled.

It is helpful to find out the direction of the ocean if the course is within a few miles of it, or to look for the highest peak if there are mountains nearby.

The challenge is that the effects from distant landscape features aren't obvious. Mountains don't square off at their bottoms onto a perfectly level field. There is a gradual sloping away from the base, so that even seemingly flat land that is miles away from the foothills has a slight, imperceptible tilt away from the mountains.

Water always seeks the lowest level, and it is common knowledge that putts will tend to break toward a greenside lake or pond. What can't readily be seen is how coastal areas of land slope subtly toward the ocean, even if the ocean is miles away. The whole course will slope in the direction of the ocean.

For each hole, look at how water might drain from the green. Modern golf course architects design greens so that water will run off in particular spots. All putts in a section of a green will tend to break toward the runoff point.

Always read your putts from the biggest view to the smallest. Look at the overall lay of the land, the high and low points around the green, the contours around the path between the ball and the hole, and finally the area of the last few feet of the putt. Let all that information percolate in your mind until an image arises that is your best guess of how the ball will make its journey toward the hole.

PRACTICE EXERCISE:

The following technique will help improve your green-reading skills. It uses your imagination to change your perception. Set a ball about twenty feet from a hole on a relatively flat portion of green. Cup your hands on each side of your eyes to create blinders for a tunnel-vision effect, so that you see only a few feet to either side of the path between ball and hole. The part of the green you see will look rather level.

Take your hands away and soften your gaze so that your peripheral vision opens up far to your left and right, while still looking in the direction of the hole. Imagine as vividly as you can that there is a mountain just to the left of the green, and a lake just to the right of the green. Notice the subtle shift in how you see the surface of the green. You will likely perceive a very slight tilt away from the mountain and toward the lake. To test it, go back to the tunnel vision, seeing the green as level, then open to wide peripheral vision, this time imagining the reverse: a mountain on the right and a lake on the left. Notice the difference in your perception of how the green slopes between one imaginary landscape and the other.

If you know about distant mountains or bodies of water that are subtly affecting the slope of the greens, imagine that feature to be near the green so that your perception of the break is influenced in the appropriate way. It may be a very subtle effect, but awareness of the lay of the land when you read the green can make the difference between a putt that barely misses and a putt that rolls right into the center of the cup.

Putting Near a Bunker

A subtle aspect of the lay of the land concerns the area of the green nearest a greenside bunker. Day after day, golfers explode sprays of sand out of the bunker and onto the green. Most of it lands within a few feet of the fringe. Essentially, that area is top-dressed with sand every day the way a greenskeeper does every few months. The sand settles in and becomes part of the green. After several years, the sand accumulates enough to raise the surface of the green along the side near the bunker. The slope away from the fringe becomes a bit steeper than the original design.

When the path of your putt passes near a greenside bunker, take the sanding of the green into account and play for the putt to break away from the bunker a little more than you'd expect.

Gravity

Think of a roulette wheel. The croupier starts the ball rolling speedily along the upper rim of the wheel. It circles around, time after time, seemingly defying gravity. It is only when the ball slows down that it falls into one of the slots in the base of the wheel. The influence of gravity depends on the speed the ball is rolling.

In the same way, the faster the ball rolls on the green, the less the slope of the surface will affect its direction. That's why golfers say, "I hit it through the break," when the putt doesn't curve as much as they thought it would because it approaches the hole at a faster pace than intended. On the other hand, the slower the ball rolls, the more it will turn downslope from the effect of gravity. That's why they say, "It didn't hold its line," when the putt falls off below the hole because it slows down sooner than intended.

It is helpful to recognize that gravity affects the path of uphill and downhill putts differently. For downhill putts, gravity will make every putt seek a similar direction, like all the tributaries of a river turning in the direction of the main river flowing downstream. As water does, they all seek the lowest point of the green. Downhill putts will hold their line, because gravity will make them tend to flow in a single direction. For your downhill putt, visualize it just trickling over the front edge of the hole. Gravity is on your side to keep the putt on path, and this way you won't have a very long second putt if your first misses the hole.

As uphill putts slow down, they will tend to veer off of their line, because gravity will make them try to turn back downhill in any direction they can, like a fountain in which the water shoots straight up, but then turns in every direction as it returns downward, creating the circular plume you see. That's why you might observe one person's rather straight uphill putt turn slightly to the right and the next one turn to the left.

Although we may fear having too long a putt coming down a steep green if we send our uphill putt too far past the hole, we need to balance that concern with the likelihood of our first putt veering off of the path we send it on. If you try to trickle it in, you have gravity working against you, turning the ball away from the hole. It is better to visualize your uphill putt going firmly into the back of the cup. Think of the steep slope as a backstop, trusting that your ball won't go very far past the hole if it misses on the way up.

You'll do a better job of reading the green by using your feet as well as your eyes. Our bodies can sense the pull of gravity, perhaps more precisely than our eyes can judge how level the surface is. As you walk between the ball and the hole, you can feel how gravity will affect the break and pace of your putt by how much you are pulled to one side or another, and how much uphill or downhill it feels.

Understanding gravity from a big perspective, we can factor in the subtle effects of the lay of the land as we read a putt. We can use our eyes to see the contour of the green's surface, and feel the slopes with our bodies as we walk. Most important of all is our attitude toward gravity. We can think of gravity as an ally instead of an enemy and use it to our advantage. Rather than feeling like we have to hold the line against gravity as we putt, we can play for plenty of break and rely on gravity to turn it as it rolls. We can think of gravity as a partner, freeing us to commit to sending the ball along the path we've chosen, and trusting that our teammate gravity will pull it toward the hole.

Grain

The grain of the greens, the direction in which grass leans as it grows, affects the speed and break of putts. You can identify the direction of the grain by the sheen of the surface. When it looks dark and dull, you are looking into the grain; when light and shiny, you are looking with the grain. Another way to iden-tify the direction of the grain is to look at the edge of the hole. The side that is ragged is the direction toward which the grain runs, because you're seeing the cut roots of the grass leaning away from the hole. The other side of the hole has the tops of the grass lying across the edge because they are leaning toward the hole. In general, the grain is likely to run toward the setting sun and toward nearby water.

Bermuda grass greens are subject to more effect of the grain than bent grass, but the putting on any green that isn't quite fast and smooth will be influenced to some extent by grain.

One mental game challenge of grain is that you have to stroke a level putt as if it were uphill when putting into the grain, and as if it were downhill when putting with the grain. This means finding a way to override the instinct to act accord-ing to your perception.

For putts that are directly into or with the grain, visualize the pace at which you'd like the ball go in the hole, as you would for an uphill or downhill putt. When putting into the grain, visualize the ball going firmly into the back of the cup. When putting with the grain, visualize the ball just trickling over the front edge of the cup.

Putting across the grain is trickier. The slower the putt is rolling, the more the grain will influence the direction. Commit to making firmer short putts to reduce the impact of the grain on the break. For longer putts, the influence of the grain growing across an otherwise straight putt can be challenging. It's hard to play for break on what looks like a level putt. You need to commit to aiming away from the middle of the hole, trusting that the grain will turn the ball toward the hole as it rolls. You can use visualization to make it easier to make that commitment. Visualize a ridge in the green on the side of your putt from which the grain is growing. Start the putt a bit toward the imagined ridge, trusting the putt will break away from it toward the hole. Or you can imagine a strong wind blowing across the surface in the direction of the grain, and trust that it will push the ball to one side as it rolls. Either of these images will cause your intuitive mind more easily to see the putt breaking, despite the apparently level surface, and you will be better able to rely on the grain to move the putt in the direction you expect.

In general, the slower the greens, the more impact the grain will have. As you gain more experience putting on grainy greens, you'll better understand how grain affects the paths of different kinds of putts.

Perpendicular Putts

Most people know to "go to school" when one of their fellow competitors is putting before them from the same direction as their putt. They watch to get more information on how their own putt might break. However, few people realize that they can also learn from observing a putt on a path that is perpendicular to their own. How those putts react to the green around the hole provides valuable knowledge about what will happen near the end of your putt.

Watch the perpendicular putt as it nears the hole. If it breaks toward your ball, you know that your putt is uphill as it approaches the hole. If the putt breaks away from your ball, your putt will be going downhill at the hole.

If the perpendicular putt slows as it approaches the hole, the end of your putt will break in the direction that putt came from. If the perpendicular putt keeps its pace as it goes by the hole, then as your putt nears the hole, it will break in the direction that putt was heading.

Perpendicular putts can give you the little bit of extra information that could mean holing a putt you would otherwise have missed, which makes them well worth watching.

As a drill, work your way around in a circle, rolling ten-foot putts at three-foot intervals. Notice how the break changes subtly from putt to putt. Before long you'll be able to go to school on any putt from any direction.

Take the High Road

When facing a steep sidehill putt that looks as if it will break a substantial amount, play for the maximum amount of break that will allow the ball to reach the hole on the high side. If the ball doesn't go in, you will likely have a short, low-stress second putt. If you play for less break and the putt misses below the hole, the ball usually runs out quite a bit farther than when it misses above the hole.

Reading for maximum break is a skill that you can develop through experience. Start by going to the far side of the hole and below it, looking back up along the possible directions from which a ball coming down the hill would most likely roll straight toward the hole. Track backward from there up the hill, until you come to the apex of the path. That is the point at which the ball starts to turn and roll downhill toward the hole. Then determine the path the ball needs to take to get to the apex.

To judge the pace the ball needs in order to roll the full length of the putt, make your best guess as to how big a stroke to make for the ball to reach the apex of your intended path, and then add on just a little for it to go the rest of the way. It's all downhill from there.

Practice putting sidehill putts with various amounts of break until you find the middle-way path that's not too high, not too low, but just right.

PRACTICE EXERCISES:

An ordinary scorecard can be used as a helpful training aid. Lay the card so that it covers half the hole, with the edge of the card going across the center on a line pointing straight at the ball, and with the open half of the hole on the high side for your putt. Practice reading your putts so that you choose a path that gives your putt the best chance of going in the open half of the hole.

You can also improve your ability to read big breaking putts by using a long drinking straw. Go behind the hole and lay the straw across the middle of the hole, with the straw pointing toward the ball and extending along the ground a few inches on either side of the hole. Imagine the putt rolling toward the hole on a path with a lot of break. As it turns and nears the hole, the ball will go in only on the high side of the straw; a ball coming on the other side will break below the hole. Swivel the straw toward the side from which the ball will be breaking until you feel that the ball would go in on either side of the straw. You now have the *through path* of the putt. The point where the straw touches the near edge of the hole is the *effective center* of the hole. See the putt entering the hole at that point on its edge, and track the curving path back and forth between that point on the hole and the ball. Start your putt on that path, and see if it can roll in on either side of the straw. Adjust your read until you find the ideal through path and effective center.

Split the Difference

Occasionally when golfers read a putt from behind the ball and then go behind the hole, the break they see looks very different. In some cases, it actually looks as if the putt breaks in the opposite direction. Which read should we choose?

Obviously two different reads of the same putt can't both be correct. There is an optical illusion functioning here. The distortion is based on the difference in what you perceive when you're looking from two different directions. The distortion seems to be accentuated when the putt is steeply uphill or downhill. When we look at the same path from two different directions, we also see the area of the green around the path, and our peripheral vision subconsciously includes the rest of the green and even the lay of the land into the distance. Looking from opposite directions means seeing two different landscapes. The different visual cues that affect our judgment can produce very contradictory impressions.

From my experience, the best thing to do is to split the difference. If it looks as if the putt will break a lot when viewed from behind the ball but very little when looking from behind the hole—or vice versa—split the difference and play the path of the break to be halfway between the two.

When it looks as if the putt will break slightly one way from behind the hole and slightly the opposite way from behind the ball, it may mean there are two subtle breaks in each direction, or no break at all. Either way, the best strategy in that situation is to set up with the putter face aimed at the middle of the hole and make a good stroke with the pace you want.

No matter what path you decide to play, it is critical that you make a firm commitment to sending the ball down that path. Leaving doubt in your mind can produce second-guessing as you swing, resulting in a tentative stroke and a poor roll. Tell yourself that you are going to swing the putter on the path you've chosen, and can deal with however it turns out.

Falling in Love with the Line

Sometimes you see golfers taking a long time looking over their putt, squatting and squinting, trying hard to be sure they are choosing the right path. When it finally comes time to roll it, they leave it well short of the hole.

We become so absorbed in trying to figure out the break and choosing the path for our putt that we forget about the pace. When we leave the putt short, we say, "I fell in love with the line and forgot to hit the putt."

The remedy for that habit is to gather yourself after you're done reading the putt and remind yourself of the three components of making a putt: path, pace, and roll. The commitment to pace as well as path is essential for holing putts. Generate an image of how fast you want the ball to be rolling as it enters the cup, and get a feel for the size of swing that will produce that pace. Take a full breath and go through your routine, executing your stroke for the pace you want in the direction of the path that you so carefully chose.

Pour, Trickle, and Pop

When faced with a putt of consequence for the match, it is not unusual to hear your playing partner say "Don't leave it short," or "Make sure you get it there." While they may regard it as a helpful reminder, it can often cause more harm than good. That's also true when we say or think those words to ourselves.

Consciously thinking harder or softer, long or short, makes your body act in an exaggerated way. The thought of making sure you get it there could end up with you sending it six feet past the hole. That's what I call a very good job of not leaving it short. But not such a good job of making the putt. It is better to refrain from giving yourself those instructions as you're about to putt. Instead, use visualization to make subtle adjustments in the size of your stroke. It works for putts that are uphill or downhill, into or with the grain, or on greens that are faster or slower than you're used to.

For putts that are uphill or into the grain, or on particularly slow greens, you want to feel comfortable making a bigger stroke than you're used to for level putts of that distance. If you picture the ball popping firmly into the back of the cup, it will feel natural to make a bigger stroke. Another image that may be helpful, if you have the tendency to leave those kinds of putts short, starts with reading the putt and seeing how the path would continue if the hole were covered and the ball rolled across it. The image of this "through path" lets you project how far the ball would roll past the hole on the path you've chosen.

Picture it rolling one foot "through" the hole. Looking beyond the hole gives your intuitive mind an image of a slightly longer putt. That will translate into your body making a slightly bigger stroke, without you consciously directing it to do so. You'll have no concern about the one-footer coming back if you miss, and it will give you the freedom to let the putter head make a big enough swing to get the ball rolling all the way to the hole.

For putts that are downhill or with the grain, or on particularly fast greens, imagine the ball just trickling over the edge of the cup. That image lets your body know that you're okay with a smaller swing than you're used to making for level putts of that distance.

Deciding on the way you want the ball to go in the hole—pour, trickle, or pop—brings various benefits and risks into play. If the ball is rolling at a slow enough pace to just trickle in when it gets to the hole, then the putts that hit the edge of the cup are more likely to fall in. That makes the effective size of the hole larger. However, at a slower pace, the inconsistencies in the putting surface more easily influence the ball to send it off its path, especially if the green adjacent to the hole is slightly crowned or it's late afternoon after there has been a lot of foot traffic around the hole.*

If the ball is rolling at a fast enough pace to pop into the back of the hole, then the inconsistencies in the putting surface are less likely to influence the ball and send it off its path.

---

* A crowned hole means that the area immediately around the opening is raised. This is a consequence of the surface around the hole not being pressed down enough after the plug of earth and sod is pulled out to make the hole. Footprints pressing down a circle a few inches from the hole cause a circular indentation and contrasting raised area next to the hole. This is what Dave Pelz calls the "lumpy donut" effect.

However, putts that hit the edge of the cup are more likely to lip out. That makes the effective size of the hole smaller. If the ball is rolling at a pace to pour into the hole, not too fast and not too slow, you get some of the benefit and some of the risk of the other approaches.

Make your choice, pre-accept the balance of benefits and risks that go with your choice, and commit to rolling the ball at that pace.

PRACTICE EXERCISE:

Practice rolling the same putt into the hole at three different paces—popping into the back, pouring into the middle, trickling over the front edge. First, find the pace you feel most comfortable with on a medium-length, relatively flat putt. Then try different paces for a variety of putts: sidehill, uphill, downhill, short, and long. For each kind of putt, determine the pace that gets you the best result while still enabling you to pre-accept the risk.

Soften Your Gaze

Softening your gaze over a putt means relaxing your vision to include a wider area, rather than focusing tightly only on the ball. To widen your field of vision, you have to relax the tension in the facial muscles around your eyes. When the muscles around your eyes soften, there's a natural spread of relaxation to other nearby muscles. Your jaw, neck, shoulders, and arms start to relax, even down to a subtle softening of your hold on the putter.

A soft gaze helps your target awareness on short putts. Without moving your eyes you can see the hole toward one side of your wider field of vision. You can even follow the roll of the ball all the way to the hole without moving your eyes. Since you can already see the hole, there's no need to look up to see if the ball goes in. That helps keep your head steady on short putts.

Bud was a touring pro who asked me to work with him on short putts. He was often one shot from making or missing the cut at his tour events. He felt pressure not to lose a stroke when he had a short putt left to save par or to miss an opportunity when he had one to make birdie. That translated into high tension over short putts, and he was missing a lot of them.

Bud feared that he'd miss the putt if he didn't make perfect contact with the ball. That made him get caught up in the mechanics of his putting stroke, as well as grip the putter too tightly. The fear also caused him to focus his eyes sharply on the ball, which tightened his face and neck muscles. All that tension made a smooth rhythmic stroke next to impossible. In addition, he was so concerned about the results of his putt that he would often come out of his stance to look toward the hole before he completed his stroke, causing him to mishit the putt. With all that interference, it's no wonder he missed a lot of short putts. Missing them only intensified the fear, and made him more uptight.

I taught Bud how to soften his gaze to help him release the tension and free him of the need to turn toward the hole to see his results on short putts. He was immediately more relaxed over his putts, felt more steady, and started holing more putts.

PRACTICE EXERCISE:

You can include softening your gaze in your putting routine for every putt. To practice this, take your putting stance and address a ball about six feet from a hole.

Look toward the ball, but widen the focus of your eyes so that you see more of your field of vision, especially side to side. You'll need to relax the tension in the facial muscles around your eyes. Feel the difference in the amount of tension in those muscles by alternately tightening and softening your focus. Tight focus, tight muscles.

You may find it helpful to synchronize the softening of your gaze with a gentle exhalation of a settling breath.

Notice that your awareness covers a wide area of the green, including the hole. Without moving your eyes, direct most of your attention toward the hole. Then just let your arms swing and send the ball toward that target. While keeping your head steady, practice following the ball out to the side of your field of vision as it rolls along its path to the hole.

Merging Vision
and Visualization

Jan is a tour player who told me that he likes softening his gaze when he is about to putt. He feels more comfortable putting toward a target he can see. For the short putts, up to about eight feet, he can see all the way to the hole out of the corner of his eye. He also finds it easy to keep his head steady, since he feels no need to look up to see where the ball is going. But outside of eight feet, he finds it harder to see the hole, and he can't see much of anything for longer putts. He wanted to know what he should do about his gaze for longer putts.

When you soften your gaze, your field of vision extends farther to each side than you might imagine. Looking straight ahead, most people have peripheral vision awareness for a full 180 degrees (a semicircle extending straight out to the left and right), sometimes a bit more. Its span is determined by the widest angle from which light can enter your eye. This means that when you set up over a putt and are looking down toward the ground, your field of vision extends out to the horizon. If you're on flat enough land, you can even get a glimpse of the sky!

If we can see the sky, why can't we see the hole on a long putt? Actually, distance to the hole isn't the issue. The hole going out of focus is the problem.

The area a few feet in every direction from the point you are looking toward is in sharp focus. That's why Jan could see the hole on short putts pretty well out to about eight feet away. Beyond that, the focus of the visual image gets progressively less and less sharp. At the far reaches of your peripheral vision there is just a vague sense of colors and tones, like glimpsing the sky in the distance. That makes it hard to distinguish the hole from the general color of the green. To add to the challenge, the farther away the hole is, and the closer your eyes are to the ground (as when you bend down into your putting stance), the less the hole is a circle and the more it appears as a narrow oval slit. That's why your caddie or playing partner is allowed to tend the flagstick as you putt.

The solution I taught Jan was to merge his vision with his visualization, and it can work for you, too. As part of your routine, visualize the path of the putt all the way to the hole from behind the ball, with a definite point on the edge of the hole over which you intend the ball to roll. Repeat this again when you've settled into your putting stance. Do so by turning your head—without lifting and turning your body—and looking along the path of the putt all the way out to the hole. Look at that for a couple of seconds, imprinting the image in your mind. When you look back down toward the ball, soften your gaze and direct your awareness toward the hole, along the path you pictured. Merge your visualization of the hole with your peripheral vision.

You are combining actual and remembered perceptions. You have a general sense of the green, not in sharp focus. Your memory adds the details of the hole, and how far it is from you, to your vague perception of the side of your field of vision. The memory of what you saw is overlaid onto the green extending into the distance. The farther away the hole is, the more you need your visualization to supplement the actual visual image. How clearly you can merge vision and visualization depends on the sharpness of your imagination in remembering what you saw when you looked directly at the path and hole. That's where training comes in. You can train your ability to soften your gaze and visualize expansively by practicing the "Panoramic Awareness" exercise on pages 55–56. The more you've trained your mind, the clearer image you'll have of the path to the hole, and the better chance you'll have of the putt ending up there.

Small Targets, Small Misses

If your target is the hole in general, when you miss your target the putt doesn't go in. If your target is a tiny point on the edge of the hole, the effective center of the path the ball will take as it approaches the hole, you can miss your target by two inches on either side and still hole the putt. The same applies for choosing a target with your driver. If your target is "anywhere in the fairway," a miss leaves you in the rough. If your target is a point on the fairway, you can miss your target by twenty yards in either direction and still have a good lie.

Another reason to pick a specific target is that the more precise an image you have in your mind, the better job your body will do at producing the image your mind gives it. Vague target, vague swing. Sharp image, sharp swing.

It is an irony of golf that it is helpful to pick a precise target but it is also helpful to have in mind a feeling of pre-acceptance for a wide range of results. Golfers have to hold the paradoxical attitude of believing they will send the ball to a specific target every time while recognizing that realistically they have a dispersion pattern and therefore will often miss their target. Ben Hogan, one of the all-time great ball strikers, said that if he hit the exact shot he intended three times during a round, it was a good round of golf. The best strategy is to choose a small target that leaves you plenty of margin for error for your small misses.

Give It a Chance

There's an interesting misconception regarding a common expression: giving the putt a chance. You may have picked it up from television commentators, usually following a putt that rolls five or six feet past the hole, saying, "He must have felt that he had to give that one a chance." The misconception is

that you should hit the putt with extra pace so that you guaran-
tee it won't stop short of the hole. If you send a putt at too fast a
pace, are you really giving it a chance?

Unfortunately, when the ball is traveling at a speed that
takes it more than two feet past the hole, your chances of holing the putt are worse, not better. Studies by Dave Pelz have
shown that putts have the best chance of going into the hole
when they are traveling at a pace such that, if the hole were
covered, they would roll a foot or two past it, not more. Also,
the chances of missing the comebacker increase as the ball
goes farther and farther past the hole.

The problem with thinking that you have to give it a little
extra is the tendency to hit it harder or take a much bigger
stroke. Any thoughts of giving it something extra or worrying
about leaving it short are unhelpful interference. That takes
you out of your tempo and flow. As you swing, if you make an
extra big stroke, you could panic on the way to the ball, decelerate, and end up leaving the putt short. If you take a normal
swing but then fear not hitting it hard enough as the putter
comes back to the ball, you could hit harder at it and send it
rolling by. Too much thinking and you just get in your own way.

The best way to give it a chance is to stay with your routine,
and putt it like you'd putt any other putt. The only adjustment
you might make would be in your picture of how the ball will
enter the hole. Visualize the ball pouring into the cup instead of
trickling in on a downhill putt. See it going quite firmly into the
back of the cup on a level or uphill putt. Read a little less break
than you would for a putt that dies into the hole. Pre-accept the
possibility of a longer comebacker than usual. Go through your
regular routine, and do your best to make the putt you intend
with your best roll, pace, and path. Look for it to go in just the
way you pictured it.

Rehearsing Your Stroke

In my golf schools, the question of taking a practice or re-hearsal stroke often comes up. The answer is that it's up to you. If you watch the pros, you'll see that some take practice strokes and some don't. Practice strokes have different purposes, re-flected in the names that describe them: tempo swing, feel swing, programming swing, rehearsal swing, and so on. We'll look at different styles for making a practice stroke so you can decide if, where, when, and how you might incorporate them into your putting routine.

The first option to consider is the simplest: Don't take a practice swing. If you have confidence in your putting-to-nowhere stroke and your feel for the pace of the greens, you may prefer to just do your routine and stroke the putt without a practice swing.

If you do take a practice stroke, the purpose you have in mind is an important part of your choice. Tempo and feel swings are used primarily to relax the arms and hands, get a feel for the weight of the putter head, and warm up to the tempo of your swing motion. The size of the swings you make isn't usually a priority.

Programming swings have the purpose of reinforcing a particular feeling or movement that you've been working on to make it a more ingrained habit in your putting stroke, such as making your follow-through at least as big as your backswing, or holding your finish, etc. Consider the move "programmed in" so that you don't need to consciously think about it during your real putting stroke.

Rehearsal swings are intended to preview the precise stroke you want to make. It is important to make individual, actual putting strokes from start to finish. Make your rehearsal swings until they are the tempo and size you feel will produce the putt you envision. Address the ball and reproduce what you rehearsed.

Some golfers look along the path to the hole while making their practice stroke. As you look at the hole, get a feel for how big a swing you need to make to send the ball that far. Commit to making that size stroke when you putt. If you use this technique, be sure to take your practice swings far enough from the ball to keep from accidentally hitting it.

The most common place you see players taking their practice stroke is next to the ball. Another choice is behind the ball. If you make your practice stroke there, do so looking past the ball toward the hole. Continue your routine by taking a full breath in preparation for walking forward into your address.

Some players have a set number of swings they like to take. The benefit is consistency in the flow of the routine, but there is also the danger of becoming too rigid, to the point of superstition. I recommend having the intention to keep your routine consistent, while maintaining the flexibility of taking an extra swing or two if the situation and your intuition call for it.

There is no right or wrong; experiment with different practice stroke routines until you find the one that is most comfortable and helps you to be the most consistent.

Get the Ball Rolling:
Structuring Your Putting
Routine

In golf, every shot is new and different. Our ability to make a confident, free swing is encouraged by trust. We trust when we feel comfortable in a situation, and we feel most comfortable when the situation is familiar. In an ever-changing setting, we can find familiarity in our routine.

Routine means customary; doing things in the usual way. Repeat the same process for every putt and you'll feel like the situation is more familiar, therefore more trustworthy. Routine fosters consistency.

In addition to making the situation familiar, a good routine establishes an even tempo and good setup habits. Following are the components I recommend for a putting routine. There is no one way that's right for everyone. Find the elements that work for you, and make them truly routine by continually practicing your putting routine on and off the course.

Reading Routine

Reading the putt on a particular green starts before you ever get to the green. Start with the widest view. Remember any pattern of influence like mountains or ocean that affects all the greens, and within that context look at the lay of the land.

As you get to the green, look for high and low points around the edges. Look for the fall line in the area of the hole, the direction that all putts will move toward.

Once you've marked your ball, stand behind your mark and survey the general path to the hole. Get your first intuitive flash of the path the putt is likely to take. If in doubt after looking more carefully, rely on your first impression.

Refine your read by walking between ball and hole, using your feet to feel for slope. Decide on the *effective center* of the hole, the point you expect the putt to roll across on the edge of the cup. Visualize your path, working backward from that point on the hole to your ball marker.

Replace your ball. If you use a line on the ball, align it with the start of your path.

Approach Routine

Stand a few steps behind the ball and move your eyes along the path at the speed you expect the putt to roll. Make a commitment to that path and pace. Select a small intermediate target a foot or two in front of the ball, if that technique is helpful to your alignment. Take a full breath, and let it flow out slowly and completely.

The completion of an exhalation is one of the most important components in your putting routine, as well as in your routine for every golf shot. There is a particularly potent feeling of settling and grounding at the end or bottom of the outbreath. Many golfers take a full breath behind the ball, but start forward too quickly. They don't let the breath flow all the way out, so they miss the value of settling and centering before moving into their address.

In the rhythm of your routine, when you are looking down the path from behind the ball, let your outbreath completely finish, and just feel yourself settle for a moment. Only then should you start to walk forward to address the ball and take your stance, letting the breath flow back in naturally, and feeling the ground as you walk.

Some golfers have told me that they take another full breath to feel settled, centered, and softened just before they start their stroke. The completion of the outbreath is their signal to let their arms start the putter in motion. I offer this for you to explore for yourself. Please keep in mind that this adds another stage to your routine, and is not for everyone.

Address Routine

Set the putter face behind the ball, perpendicular to the start of your path. Lean in to set your spine angle, move your feet into position and take your stance.

Look again along the path to the hole, moving your eyes at the pace you intend the putt to roll. This is the time to be certain you are committed to the path and pace you've chosen. If you have second thoughts, take a step back out of your stance to clear your mind of doubt. If you can't shake the uncertainty, look the putt over again, commit to your read, and return to your approach and address routines.

Stroking the Putt

Having committed to your path and pace, soften your gaze when you look back down at the ball. Be aware of the path leading to the hole, merging your visualization of the hole with your peripheral vision for longer putts. Let a feeling of softening flow down your shoulders and arms to your hands, dissolving any tension. As mentioned earlier, some golfers let another breath go all the way out as a further settling process.

Let your arms swing the putter back and through. Hold the finish for a second, then turn your head to look and see how the putt rolled out.

Of all the elements of the routine presented to this point, choose the combination that works best for you. None are absolutes, although finishing the outbreath before walking forward is highly recommended.

Post-Putt Routine

If you did not make the putt you intended and you get upset, give yourself a moment to get over it. Take another full breath and let it all the way out to clear any strong emotional reaction. Then objectively reflect on how you may have gotten in your own way, or misjudged the path or pace. Learn what you can and let it go.

Step to the side and reenact the putt as you would have preferred to execute it. That clears the negativity and frees you from concern about technique when you face your next putt.

If you made the putt, feeling good about the roll, pace, and path, you can use the experience to reinforce your process, saying, "That's the way I always putt when I get out of my own way." You're giving yourself the message that high-quality execution is your ordinary way of putting.

Summary of a Putting Routine

- Read the putt, going from wide view to narrow.
- Standing a few paces behind the ball, picture your path.
- If you take a practice stroke, do so here or just before you address the ball.
- Complete your outbreath and settle, then feel the ground as you walk forward.
- Set the putter face behind the ball with a soft grip, then set your stance.
- Look along your path and recommit to it.
- Soften your gaze, soften your arms, and let the putter swing.
- Hold your finish, hold your posture, then turn your head to look.
- Reflect on quality of execution and learn from the results.

As mentioned earlier, you can design your putting routine to include the elements that best suit you. Explore different routines to find one with natural flow and tempo, that is easily repeatable, and that helps you set up to each putt with clarity, commitment, and composure.

PART 6

Up to the Challenge

In order to overcome hesitation and commit, a leap is necessary. The way to be daring, the way to leap, is to disown the ups and downs of your thoughts and step beyond your hope and fear.

—Venerable Chögyam Trungpa,
Shambhala: The Sacred Path of the Warrior

Why We Leave Putts Short

Every golfer knows the saying, "Never up, never in." So why do we leave putts short when we know that it makes it impossible to hole them? Everyone does it, and it's possible for everyone to do it less. Let's take a look at the variety of reasons why golfers leave putts short, and what can be done to remedy the situation.

One simple reason is misjudgment of the speed of the green. If you started the putt at the pace you intended, but the putt ended up short, you misjudged the speed of the green. Was the putt more uphill, or less downhill, than you thought? If so, what didn't you notice about the lay of the land? Was the putt more into the grain or less with the grain than you thought? Was this green slower than those on the preceding holes? Look at the grass more carefully. Learn all you can from every putt so that you'll be better at judging speeds.

We also leave putts short if we become so preoccupied with choosing the best path for the putt that we forget to attend to the pace required. That's when we utter the painful cry, "I forgot to hit it!" The remedy is a strong routine, remembering to establish an intention for the size of the stroke and the pace of the putt, including a vivid picture of the ball pouring into the cup.

Perhaps the most common cause of leaving putts short is trying to be too perfect, too careful. You tighten up and make a restricted stroke. Hope of holing the putt makes you try to guide the ball instead of swinging the putter. Fear of not holing the putt makes you decelerate as you swing. This lack of freedom means a smaller stroke in addition to less speed through impact, and the putt ends up woefully short. The best remedy is to get over thinking about what the putt is for and rely on your routine. Focus on your process and it will be less likely that concern for results interferes with your stroke.

If you have doubts about the pace or the path you've chosen, you might hold back during your swing for fear of making a mistake. Hesitation in the mind becomes deceleration in the stroke, which means the putt ends up short. The remedy for deceleration is to strengthen your commitment to the pace, path, and swing you've chosen. Commit to it with pre-acceptance of the results, confident that you can handle whatever happens. If you are free from hope and fear about how the putt will turn out, you won't decelerate.

Another form of interference that causes us to leave putts short is our fear of three-putting. We get ahead of ourselves, worrying about the putt we'll have left if we go too far past the hole. Putting uphill, we worry about going too far past the hole and leaving ourselves a tricky downhill slider. Putting downhill, we worry about it getting away from us and rolling out to leave a long comebacker. Either way, we make a very tentative stroke. The result is usually the exaggerated opposite of what we feared.

Sometimes we are influenced by another person's putt. We get scared of the green being extra fast on the path we're putting when our partner or fellow competitor runs his putt or chip well by the hole. Lee Trevino, a major champion, once unintentionally rolled a long putt well past the hole. Instead of acknowledging his error, he said, "Whew, that green is slick. I hardly touched it." His opponent, who had a putt on a similar path, left his five feet short.

Finally, leaving a putt short can be a subtle way of protecting our ego. We know we'll feel badly if the ball goes by the hole and doesn't go in. If it goes by the hole, we can't deny the fact that we missed the hole. However, if we leave the putt short, if it never reaches the hole, we can say, "I would have made it if I'd just hit it a little firmer." In a subtle mental manipulation to protect our ego, we tell ourselves that we didn't really miss the hole—we just left it short.

Hold Your Finish

Jason had qualified for his first PGA Tour event of the year, securing one of only four spots contested by over one hundred golfers. I saw him Tuesday on the putting green and asked how it was going. He said, "Just so-so." I remarked that since he qualified with a very low score, he must have been putting well. He said that in the qualifier he hit a lot of approach shots close to the hole and luckily didn't have many left-to-right putts. They were giving him fits.

I asked if there were a pattern to his misses. He said that mostly he left them below the hole, but sometimes missed them by quite a bit on the high side. I asked him to roll a few left-to-right breaking putts. As a right-handed golfer he was pushing putts toward the hole, which caused them to miss on the low side. He got preoccupied with the hole, neglected the path, and subconsciously swung the putter toward the hole.

After missing several on the low side without understanding why, he reacted by not trusting his read. As he started his stroke, he would add some break by pulling it up the path, sending it a bit left of the direction he originally aimed.

Pulls and pushes alternated, and he was caught in a cycle of compensation, first thinking he was playing too much break, then thinking he was playing too little, never realizing he was pushing and pulling the putts.

I explained the cycle he was experiencing, and suggested that it would help him feel it for himself by exaggerating what he was doing. I asked him to aim at the hole and pull it left, then aim well left of the hole and push it toward the hole. Alternating these helped him recognize and feel how he was altering his swing path from his originally intended direction. Then I asked him to take a couple of practice strokes, with the special instruction of holding his finish.

Holding your finish means leaving the putter head in position for a second or two after it has reached its farthest extension forward in the stroke. Jason wasn't comfortable holding a poor finish position. He could clearly see that he had either manipulated the direction of the swing path, turned the putter face, or both. Knowing that he would be accountable for the quality of his stroke, he immediately became more consistent in maintaining his swing path.

When your intuitive mind knows you will be holding the finish, that you will be accountable for your quality of execution, it also knows how to engage your body in swinging to a good finish. It will do its best to produce the optimum stroke for getting to that finish—not pushing or pulling the putt, but swinging back and through so that the putter face returns squarely to the ball and sends it along the path at which the putter face was originally aiming.

Higher handicappers most often miss on the low side because they underestimate the amount of break. After a few of those misses, they pull or push the next putt in reaction to the last one, and fall into a cycle of pushes and pulls. Hold your finish, learn from the putt, and start to play enough break to stay on the high side.

For golfers of all levels of ability, once you can hold your finish and know you didn't push or pull the putt, it will reveal information if your putt misses the hole. When Jason held his finish in a good position, with no push or pull, he knew that if he missed the putt, it was because of an incorrect read of the green for the break or the pace.

Jason practiced holding his finish in this way: He made a practice stroke or two and held the finish on those, then held the finish on the actual putt. He played and putted his way into the top ten that week, earning more money than he had made the entire year before.

Hold your finish and watch your putts run true and go in more often.

Turn Knee Knockers into Tap-ins

Bill, a veteran and a long-time golfer, told this story:

"During World War II, as a Marine torpedo bomber pilot, our training included a course in staying relaxed while facing fear-producing situations. We were put in a dimly lit room where we were instructed to lie on our back on a cot, hands at our sides, and go through a body scan to relax. Our instructor then stopped next to each of us and asked us a question. We were to answer promptly

and then go back to our scan without any second thoughts about our response. When it came my turn, he said, "You are flying at five hundred feet, your plane is on fire, and your engine has quit. Would you bail out at such a low altitude where your parachute probably won't open, or opt to attempt a crash landing in flames?" I don't remember my answer, but after all these years, neither of those options are as bad as trying to sink a downhill four-footer on eighteen for all the marbles."

Those four-footers are fearful for many golfers. But most people don't worry too much about an eight-inch tap-in putt. It is so taken for granted in weekend play that it's usually a gimme, one your opponents concede and you don't bother putting.

Even when you have to finish it out in a tournament, you still don't regard a tap-in as a big deal. Just step up, square your putter face, and make a simple little stroke. It seems there is rarely any guiding or hesitation on those tap-in strokes. In fact, the tap-in stroke often represents the best stroke a player makes. The putter face moves back and through the ball square to and along the path at impact, follows right through nearly to the hole, and the ball dives into the middle of the cup at a good pace.

A group of college players came to me for a lesson, and one of them said he was struggling on short pressure putts. He explained that he is usually so careful and guiding when putting those short putts that they just wobble up to the hole and barely go in if they reach it. "I feel like I'm wishing them in rather than really stroking them." I asked him to set a ball down at what was a simple tap-in for him, and knock it in. He placed the ball about eight inches from the hole and tapped it in with a nice, smooth stroke. Then I took the ball and set it three feet from the hole. I put my foot between the ball and the hole, the side of my foot about eight inches from the ball, and instructed him to make his same tap-in stroke, right into the side of my foot.

As his putter struck the ball, I pulled my foot out of the way. The ball rolled past where my foot was and continued on, pouring into the center of the cup at a very good pace.

There was a moment of silence and a stunned look on his face. "That was cool!" he exclaimed. "And it went into the hole with even more pace than my three-footers usually do. That's the pace I want them to have, going in with authority."

I pointed out that his tap-in stroke was a natural stroke with no guiding for direction, no concern about distance, no tension from fear of missing. It was also clear that his tap-in stroke carried the ball easily to the hole three feet away. Next we tested just how far his tap-in carried. We found the outline of a hole plug, where a previous hole had been, and set a ball about eight inches from the edge. I asked him to imagine that it was a real hole and play a tap-in to that hole. The ball rolled over the center of the old hole outline and continued about five feet past. I said, "This green is average in speed, not especially fast or especially slow. Your ordinary tap-in stroke will have plenty of pace for any putt up to four feet long on an average green, just three feet on a slower green, and five feet or so on a faster green."

To feel less pressure when faced with a four-foot knee knocker, turn it into a tap-in. Set up with the putter aimed at the path you intend for the putt. Focus on an imaginary hole just eight inches in front of the ball on the path toward the actual hole, and make your tap-in stroke to that imaginary hole. The key is to follow through a few inches past the ball, just as you would on an ordinary tap-in. Watch as the ball rolls along the path and into the actual hole. You just turned a four-foot knee knocker into a tap-in!

Now that "downhill four-footer on eighteen for all the marbles" doesn't have to be scarier than a parachute that might not open or a crash landing in flames. It will take a lot of the pressure off Bill when he can tell himself, "Relax, it's just a tap-in."

The Comebacker

After missing a downhill putt that runs any more than a few feet by the hole, golfers often leave the next putt, the comebacker, short of the hole. It is as if, after hitting the first putt too far, they are afraid they'll hit the second one past as well and have another tricky downhill putt.

When you hit a downhill putt that runs well past the hole, it is often hard to make the commitment to hit the putt coming back up with enough pace to reach the hole. There's a feeling of holding back, of not being able to swing freely. What is getting in the way?

First, you got feedback about your swing. Either the ball rolled farther than you thought it would with the swing you made, or you made a bigger swing than you intended. Your anxiety increased as the ball rolled farther and farther past the hole, and your subconscious mind sent a big emotional message, "TOO HARD!" It's tough to take the putter back far enough on the next putt with that thought lingering in your mind.

Second, three-putting is bad enough, but you *really* don't

want to have the ball go so far past the hole on the comebacker that you leave yourself another putt of any significant length. If you miss that one, it means a four-putt or worse. You want to swing hard enough, but not too hard. Even if you swing the putter far enough back, it's hard to swing through freely. That means deceleration, which reduces pace.

You need to clear the last putt completely from your memory. Treat the uphill comebacker as if it were your first putt on that green. The only thing that's helpful to keep in mind from the actual first putt is what you saw in the way of break after the ball rolled past the hole. That should tell you all you need to know to have a good read for the putt coming back. Think it through and bring up the most helpful images, just the way you would any uphill putt. Be sure to change your image of how you want the ball to be going into the hole. On the downhill putt, you wanted to have the image of the ball just trickling over the front edge. For the comebacker, you want to visualize the ball popping against the back wall of the cup.

Go through your routine at the same tempo you do on all your other putts. Aim the putter face and, with the image of the ball going into the back of the cup, let the putter head swing like you're putting to nowhere. When you putt that way, you give yourself the best chance to make that comebacker.

Hover to Deaden It

A steep, downhill putt of just a few feet presents an interesting dilemma. The size of swing that you would ordinarily make for that distance will send the ball far past the hole. The tendency is either to decelerate as you approach impact, or to try to make a very small stroke, a tiny jab at the ball. This usually sends the ball wobbling down the slope right from the start, with little control over pace or path.

A technique often taught to enable players to make a more normal size and tempo stroke, but not impart too much energy to the ball, is to make contact out toward the toe of the putter. Contact away from the sweet spot deadens the impact. The problem with hitting the putt toward the toe is that it can turn the face of the putter slightly open and send the ball off your intended path.

Here's an alternative technique that brings extra benefits as well. Hover the putter head off the ground so that the bottom edge is even with the middle of the ball. Contacting the ball with the bottom edge of the putter face also deadens the impact. This accomplishes the goal of reducing the amount of energy imparted while allowing a more ordinary-size stroke. But because the impact point is not off center toward the toe, the putter face won't turn at impact. Since you can make your ordinary stroke for the length of putt you face, you feel more comfortable and therefore less tense. Your stroke will naturally be more fluid when you aren't worrying about the ball going too fast for that steep, downhill putt.

One of the extra benefits of learning this technique is that if you are comfortable hovering the putter a bit off the ground, your stroke is less likely to get caught by the grass if you are putting from just off the green, or when the ball comes to rest against the fringe.

The other benefit in learning to swing while hovering the putter comes into play on windy days. According to the rules of golf, if your ball moves after you've addressed it, you receive a penalty of one stroke. In general, if you take your stance and are prepared to make a stroke, you have addressed the ball. However, when the ball is on the green, you've addressed the ball only when you've taken your stance and *grounded your club* behind the ball. If you have not grounded your club, it is not a penalty stroke if the ball moves, because you have not officially addressed it.

Hover the putter slightly when the wind is gusting enough to possibly move the ball off its spot. Hover the putter when the ball is on a very steep slope just off the green, and touching the grass behind the ball might make it move. Just slightly hovering the putter, not as much as you would to deaden a steep downhill putt, will free you from the concern of receiving a penalty stroke, while not greatly affecting the quality of contact or the pace of the putt.

It's helpful to have someone tell you where the bottom edge is in relation to the center of the ball, because almost everyone underestimates how far off the ground they are hovering the putter. Because it is an unfamiliar feeling at the last moment before swinging the putter, it is important to practice hovering the putter until you are consistent and comfortable enough to use it during a round. You'll feel more confident when you find yourself facing that steep downhill putt to save your par, and windy days won't blow you away.

Up Tiers, Down Tiers

Megan, a young tour pro, called to ask for some help with her putting in one particular situation: putting uphill on two-tiered greens. She said, "Putting downhill from one tier to another, I pick a point on the top of the hill that I think will send the ball toward the hole, putt to there, and watch it feed down the hill. Hopefully it's not going too fast as it gets near the hole. Putting up a hill from one tier to the next is much harder for me. I either barely get it over the edge or I send it zooming way past the hole."

A two-tiered green presents a special putting challenge. Each putt will start with a relatively level portion, have a steep uphill or downhill portion, and then be relatively level again. Let's look at the path and pace issues we face going up tiers and down tiers.

Putting down to a lower tier starts with reading the putt backward from the hole to the base of the hill. See where it needs to roll over the top of the slope to get to that spot at the base. Next see the path the ball will need to take to get to the point on the top edge of the slope. Roll the putt that will take you to that point, going at a pace such that the slope and lower tier add enough speed for the ball to get to the hole.

The danger here is getting too cute with the first putt, trying to be too perfect, trying to make it just barely roll over the edge. If it doesn't get there, you wasted a shot, because you still have the same putt down the slope. Better to get over the edge and deal with whatever you get on the lower tier. Sometimes all you can do is hope that it hits the hole to slow it down. But that's better than having to hope the same thing on your second putt.

Going uphill is much more challenging for both path and pace. The first portion of the putt on the lower tier will be relatively straight. The more it slows on the way up, the more the slope will affect it. Imagine the putt rolling to the base of the hill, then up across the slope to a spot where it goes over the edge of the upper tier and becomes a more level putt again.

To give the putt enough speed to get up a steep slope and then continue on to the hole, we need to make a bigger swing than we usually would for a level putt of that distance. Sometimes we're afraid of making too big a swing and the ball barely gets to the top tier, or doesn't even reach it and rolls back to our feet. On the other hand, if we guard against being short and decide to give it plenty of speed to get up the slope, we tend to overdo it and roll it far past the hole.

Perceptual distortion can cause us to underestimate the pace needed after the crest of the hill. A steep slope can make it look like the top tier is flat when in fact it continues uphill. After we clear the rise, we're surprised when the ball stops well before we expect it to.

After a couple of overly careful efforts that fell well short of the hole, Megan was determined not to be short on the next one. She gave the putt plenty of pace up the slope and it rolled far past the hole, leaving her a long second putt. On the next one she would go back to being tentative and leave it short. It was a vicious cycle, and quite a frustrating one.

I asked her to pay particular attention to the feel of rolling two different putts. First she rolled a few putts just to the top edge of the slope. Then we walked up the slope and she putted a few putts from the top of the slope to the hole.

We went back to the lower tier. I asked her to review those two feelings, reflecting on how big a swing it took to get to the top of the hill, and how big a swing it took to get from there to the hole. The plan was to let her intuition combine them for the feel of the whole putt.

The routine she was to follow was to make a practice swing of the size that would get the ball to the top of the hill, then make a practice swing of the size that would get the ball from the top of the hill to the hole. A final practice swing would add the feel of those two together. She was to address the ball and use a swing like that last practice swing to roll it up the hill and along the upper tier to the hole.

Megan looked at the whole path she intended the putt to take. She made a large practice swing for the putt up the hill, a small swing for the upper tier part of the putt, and a slightly larger swing than the first one that combined the two. Then she addressed the ball and repeated the third practice swing. The ball rolled up the hill, along the upper tier, and stopped a foot from the hole.

"Wow," was all she could say.

PRACTICE EXERCISE:

For downhill putts on a two-tiered green, practice rolling putts to an imaginary hole at the top of the tier with enough pace to safely send the putt down the slope toward the hole.

For putting up a two-tiered green, take a practice swing for the pace you need to make it up the hill, a smaller swing for the section of the putt on the upper tier, and a third swing that combines the two. Then set up to the ball, trust your intuition, and let the swing happen.

Practice this way first with putts straight up the hill to the top tier. When you feel some confidence in your sense of pace, practice putts that roll across the face of the slope at an angle. Through trial and error, learn the effects of the interaction of slope and pace to better judge at what spot the ball will emerge from the slope and in what direction it will be heading.

A particular danger in two-tiered putts comes from the tendency to get too cute with the putt, meaning that you try to make it absolutely perfect, especially by guarding against rolling it too far by the hole. Trying to be too precise usually leads to swinging the putter less freely, perhaps even decelerating at impact. The unfortunate results include leaving the downhill putt on the upper tier, or having the uphill putt not make it all the way onto the upper tier and watching it roll back to your feet. The remedy for trying to be perfect is pre-acceptance of a wider range of results. For both uphill and downhill two-tiered putts, look at the area beyond the hole and tell yourself, "I'm fine with it if it rolls a couple of feet past the hole." That will free you to make a committed stroke and give you the best chance of producing the putt you pictured.

Putting Outside the Box

Arnold Palmer's maxim for a shot just off the green was "an average putt is going to get as close as a good chip." Because of the greater quality and variety of wedges that are now available to top-tier players, chipping has a different role. The rule of thumb on the PGA Tour is: If you want to play the safest shot that you can and keep the ball close to the hole, putt; if you are trying to hole it and are willing to risk it going well past, chip. Remember that this is for players who have excellent technique and equipment, and practice extensively.

For most golfers with more than a single-digit handicap, there is a significant probability of mishitting a chip. It's usually safer to putt whenever you can. If you can get the putter on the ball without grass getting in the way and there aren't obstacles in front of you, putt.

How do you know how big a swing to make when you're a

few feet or more off the green? The ball is rolling fastest the first few feet of the putt, so the thicker grass of the fairway or fringe won't slow the ball down as much as you think unless you're much farther away. As I recommended in the previous chapter for two-tiered putts, split the putt into two parts. Make a practice swing that you think will be big enough to get through the grass to just the edge of the green. Make another practice swing that you think would roll the ball from the edge of the green to the hole. Now make a swing that combines those two, and reproduce that swing at the ball. It should get you over the thick stuff and across the green, cozying up to the hole.

What about other clubs? Experimentation is the key. Go to the short game area with all your clubs. Find out what feels most comfortable in different conditions. How far off the green are you comfortable putting? Try other clubs for this type of shot, especially hybrids or fairway woods. Choose the club that you can swing with the most confidence and gives you the most consistent results.

'Twas the Night Before Match Play

I'm often asked what mental game techniques golfers can use the night before a match or tournament as preparation to help them putt their best. Here is a mental game routine that will help you prepare for optimum putting performance in your round the next day.

Start early enough in the evening that you're not too tired

and sleepy. Sit in a quiet place and do a few minutes of mindful awareness practice to settle, center, and clear your mind.

Close your eyes and imagine you are on the first green of the course you're playing the next day. Imagine your ball in the center of the green and the hole in the back-right portion of the green. Mark your ball, and imagine yourself going through your full process of reading the putt, replacing your ball, and completing your regular putting routine. Imagine the ball rolling end over end on the path you chose at the pace you intended, finally going over the point on the edge of the hole that you had in mind, in the style you planned—trickling in, pouring in, or popping into the back of the cup.

Repeat the process in a clockwise direction, putting from the center of the green to front-right, front-left, and finally back-left hole locations. If you'd like, you can mix up the order of the holes to which you putt. Experiment and find what works best for you. If you are familiar with the course, you can choose hole locations you are likely to face, and imagine your ball on the green in places your approach is likely to land. Each putt should be imagined to roll in real time and finish in the hole.

Be mindful of your stamina—this takes mental energy, and you should continue only as long as you still feel fresh and awake. If you need to, do this practice in several sessions of three to six holes at a time. It may be tempting to try this in bed to end the evening, but you are not likely to last many holes before you fall asleep. If you have a late tee time, you can do this practice in the morning instead of or in addition to doing it the night before.

This method applies to more than putting. You can imagine yourself playing the whole course, from the first tee to the eighteenth hole. See your full process: choosing a target, planning the shot, pulling the club, going through your swing routine, swinging, and watching it fly and land just the way you pictured it. Always see yourself putting from the best place to have your approach shot land for the hole location you have in mind.

Play to the ideal spot on each green for one hole location, go through your full putting process, and see the ball finish in the hole for birdie (or eagle if you reached a par five in two in your imagination). Vary the position of the imaginary flagstick as you go through the course so that you have a variety of breaking and straight putts as well as uphill and downhill putts.

You can use this practice in your work as well. If you have a presentation to make or a meeting to run, go through the same process: Sit quietly and use mindful awareness practice to feel clear and settled, then imagine yourself going through the upcoming activity with good execution and successful outcomes.

This technique of visualizing future actions may seem to conflict with the principle of staying in the present, as well as the suggestion not to get ahead of yourself. They are not really in conflict, but are directed toward different aspects of experience. You are imagining each shot with good routine and outcome as a way of tuning in to your confidence, reinforcing your *process* through images of quality in execution leading to success. It is to free you from the interference of concern for *results* that you train yourself to continually relate to what is happening in the present moment.

Stop the Bleeding

How do you turn things around when you've been putting poorly for a few holes?

First there's the issue of what you think poor putting is. Focus on the process—are you making the putts you intend, but they are not going in the direction or finishing at the distance you thought they would? Then you don't need to change anything other than the way you're reading the break and/or the pace. Look beyond the hole if you're leaving them short, and picture them trickling in if you're hitting them too far. Try to have the putts fall in on the high side if you're missing them low. Play for them to go in near the middle of the hole if you're seeing more break than there actually is and missing on the high side.

If you aren't executing the putts you intend, go through a checklist of your mental preparation: (1) Do you have a clear picture of the path in mind for each putt? (2) Are you committing to that path each time? (3) Are you breathing so that you are settled and ready to putt? (4) Are you letting the putter swing as if you're putting to nowhere, or are you guiding, steering, or thinking about technique while you swing the putter? Prepare properly, clear the interference of trying rather than trusting, and you'll start rolling the putts better.

If your mental preparation seems good but your putts are off in direction or pace and not rolling end over end, review your setup. Check your posture, softness of grip, ball position, and aim of the putter face. Remember to breathe and soften your gaze.

If your setup seems good, review any of your tendencies that might interfere with making a good stroke. Are you coming up out of the putt to get an early peek at how it's doing? Are you tightening your grip pressure as you swing? Are you taking too big a backswing and decelerating before contact? Make a few of your putting-to-nowhere swings, keeping your body steady and grip soft, free from these or any of the other habits that may be getting in your way. Then commit to going through your routine and making that same putting-to-nowhere stroke for every putt, with the sole purpose of getting the putt off to a good start.

Patience is important as well. If you miss a few putts, get impatient and start forcing them, it could be a long day on the greens. Remember that the score is the same if you hole the putts on the back nine as if you hole them on the front. Stay focused on your process, stay consistent in your routine, and stay patient. It won't take long before you're making them and holing them, too.

All Choked Up

Toward the end of a big match, when the pressure is on, some players crumble. This extreme reaction to pressure is the phenomenon called *choking*. It is called choking because there is a physical sense of tightening up, as if there is pressure on one's chest and throat making it difficult to breathe. It comes from a heightened fear of failure. Anxiety leads to panic, and a golfer's game seems to fall apart. You feel as if you can't remember how to putt. Ironically, it is the reverse that happens.

It's not that you forget how to putt. It's that you stop trusting that you already know how to putt, and start giving yourself lessons while you're playing the game. Choking doesn't mean you don't know what you are doing. Choking is overdoing everything. You take longer in your routine. You look over your read of the putt again and again. You take extra practice strokes. You back out of your stance and recheck all the details. Your mind is racing; you are outthinking yourself.

There is a physiological overload happening at the same time. As tension and excitement increase, adrenaline starts flowing. It feels as if everything is happening more quickly. It seems like there is less time to make decisions and it is harder to get settled. Your movements get quicker and your hands get twitchy.

The antidote is to take a few full slow breaths. Full slow breathing and nervous anxiety are incompatible. The mind can generate tension in the body, but it also monitors the body for feedback. If you are breathing rhythmically and the body is settled, your mind will relax as well.

The remedy for choking is very straightforward: Focus on your process, stick to your game plan, commit to your routine, and keep breathing. Clear your mind of overthinking, calm your body from overexcitement, and go back to doing what you already know how to do.

To Yip or Not to Yip

I went to my doctor and told him I sometimes had pain in my neck. He asked me what the problem was. I turned my head to one side and said, "It hurts when I do that."

The doctor said, "Don't do that."

—HENNY YOUNGMAN, VAUDEVILLE COMEDIAN

The most famous obstacle to confidence in putting is the phenomenon known as the yips. It is so feared among golfers that many don't like to say or hear the word. If the thought of the yips gives you the willies, skip to the next chapter now.

When a golfer flinches uncontrollably just before impact, that is the yips. The ball doesn't just slightly miss the hole. It is not uncommon for a golfer with the yips to hit a three-foot putt five feet past the cup and on the next hole leave a similar three-foot putt two feet short. Besides missing the putt, the embarrassment of such a display can be mortifying.

The yips are notoriously hard to get rid of. They feel so much beyond the golfer's control that some theories regard them as a physical malady, a neurological disorder. They have caused golfers to give up hope and quit the game entirely. Golfers have resorted to extra-long putters and strange ways of gripping the putter to keep their dominant hand from taking over and flinching. Part of what makes the yips so insidious is the fact that they are reinforced in a vicious cycle. Our instinctive reaction to escape them only intensifies them.

The yips start to develop when you feel particularly bad and berate yourself for missing a short putt. It is an experience of emotional punishment, and people cringe or flinch when they anticipate a painful experience. On subsequent putts, you flinch when the ball is about to miss the hole. You start flinching earlier and earlier in the putting process until eventually you flinch as your putter head contacts the ball. It shoots off in a strange way, and a new fear is added. You're not just afraid of missing the putt, you're afraid of flinching as well. That is the start of the yips.

Another factor that makes the yips so deeply ingrained is the human tendency to use the hands, particularly the dominant hand, for control. Your dominant hand is what you rely on in the most challenging circumstances to execute the critical action. If you had to perform a delicate task in a life-or-death situation, you wouldn't use your foot or your nose or your less dominant hand. You'd use your dominant hand.

If you have fear as you swing the putter, your dominant hand will tighten and take control. For a right-handed golfer, that means the right hand tightens on the putter as the putter head is about to contact the ball. The more fear you have of making a poor stroke, the more your right hand will try to take over, as if it has a mind of its own.

It feels hopeless to those who are stuck with the yips, but there is a way out. A golfer named Larry can vouch for that.

Larry had the yips. He could hit towering drives, crisp straight irons, and had a decent short game. On the practice green he had a smooth stroke and rolled the ball well. But when we got on the first green of our playing lesson, I couldn't quite believe my eyes. He had a putt of about eight feet. He went through the same routine I saw on the putting green, took a couple of practice swings, and took his stance. And then it happened. His backswing stopped short after no more than two inches, followed by an abrupt jab at the ball. It jumped to the right and sped twenty feet away.

On the second green he had about the same length putt. Again he went through his routine. Again he made a cutoff backswing. But this time the putter stubbed into the ground as it contacted the ball. The putt went two feet and wobbled to a stop.

Larry was mortified that he couldn't make a putt, and horrified that it seemed beyond his control. Over the course of several sessions, we discovered some key pieces to the puzzle of his yips:

He was very comfortable swinging his woods and irons. But in putting he felt he had a very different stance, grip, and swing. It wasn't comfortable, and he didn't trust it.

He was very comfortable making full swings, and even had a feel for partial swings with his wedges. But in putting he had no feel for the size of the swing needed to send the ball a particular distance.

His practice putting swings were very big and energetic. He didn't have a purpose for doing them.

He was extremely attached to score and very concerned with what others thought of him.

Larry needed to feel more comfortable swinging a putter and less uncertain about how the swing translated into distance. He needed to have a meaningful routine and be more attuned to his process than worried about his results. Together we planned his improvement program:

He changed his putting grip to be more like his full swing grip, and stood a little farther from the ball to make him feel as if putting were more like swinging other clubs.

He practiced drills for feel on the putting green, helping him learn the swing sizes that would roll the ball different distances.

He worked on his rehearsal swings, just the size that would roll the ball the length of the putt he was facing. He practiced reproducing the same size swing at the ball as he made in his practice stroke.

He became more interested in how well he executed his process, and put more emotion into success in making putts than worrying about holing them.

He worked on giving himself a break and not beating himself up if he missed a putt.

Larry's assignment in our next playing lesson was to make a realistic size practice swing for the length of putt he faced. He was then to reproduce the size and tempo of his rehearsal swing as closely as he could. Success was based only on how good a job he did of repeating his rehearsal swing. It had nothing to do with how the putt ended up.

Larry was very focused on guessing the right size stroke for each putt and doing his best to reproduce it. He was determined to do a good job of that. On the sixth hole he realized that he'd forgotten to be worried about flinching. He got better at matching swing size and distance, and was snuggling his putts up to the hole. He stood up to a twelve-foot putt on the last hole, made a couple of rehearsal swings until he felt that the size was right, and took his stance. Larry reproduced that swing exactly, without a hint of a flinch, and had the biggest smile on his face when the ball poured right into the middle of the cup.

During a round of golf, the tendencies that reinforce the yips are diminished when your concern shifts from results to process. Turn your focus from the performance of the swing to the preparation. Apply nonjudgmental awareness to how well you maintain a soft hold on the club with your dominant hand. With a softer grip, it will be less likely that the dominant hand will take control and flinch at the ball.

Since the starting point of the yips involves self-punishment, the most fundamental remedy is to undo the habit of berating oneself and feeling embarrassed by poor performance. Taking ourselves too seriously feeds the yips; having a sense of humor starts to lessen their severity. This means the key to overcoming the yips is accepting them, not feeling embarrassed by them, and not trying to get rid of them. It's challenging to take such an attitude, but it is the start of turning the cycle of self-punishment and embarrassment into a cycle of building trust and confidence.

PART 7

Getting Out of Your Own Way

Never give up, never give in. Never give in to feelings of self-doubt and pettiness nor of arrogance and resentment. Never give up on the inherent basic goodness and self-worth of yourself and others.

—Vajra Regent Ösel Tendzin

Putting First Things First

In putting, as in golf and life, it usually works out best to do one thing at a time. In doing one thing at a time, it's best to put first things first.

Although the twenty-first century is one in which multi-tasking is the rule of the day, studies have shown that it isn't the most efficient way to use our brain. When participants' focus shifted from one task to two, the attention on each of the two tasks was only forty percent of the focus on the single task. Three tasks got only twenty-five percent attention each. The more we try to do at once, the less efficient we are overall. This will come as no surprise if you've been in a near accident with a car driven by someone who is also talking on a cell phone and drinking coffee.

In our putting routine, we put first things first by starting with the widest view for reading the putt and then moving step by step to the most subtle details. We make a commitment to our judgment of path and pace before we address the ball. We get ourselves settled and ready before we stroke the putt. We complete the backswing before we start the forward swing. We send the ball forward before we start to slow down the swing. We finish our stroke before we turn to look for the results. We learn what we can from the result before we go to the next shot. One thing at a time.

The points at which we shift from one phase of our process to the next are transitions where we can get in our own way if we don't properly complete the previous action. Setting up to the putt without commitment to the path gets in the way of making a free swing. Not completing the backswing interferes with our tempo. Coming up out of the putt before we complete the forward swing gets in the way of making good contact with the ball.

One of the biggest challenges in golf is making the transition from thinking mind to intuitive mind during our routine. We need to use our thinking mind to plan the putt, considering the lay of the land and other factors affecting break and speed. Only when that is properly completed, when we have clarity and commitment to the path and pace we've chosen, do we turn over control to our intuitive mind to execute the putt.

First plan with your head, and then play from your heart.

Reinforce or Refrain

If there's something you can do about the situation, if you have control, then there's no need for worrying. If there's nothing you can do about the situation, if it's beyond your control, then there's no point in worrying.

—ZEN PROVERB

We get in our own way, undermining our ability to perform, when our thinking mind interferes, when it tries to take control rather than letting the intuitive mind accomplish our intentions. If our thinking mind takes over and gives directions to our body while we're in the process of swinging the putter, it rarely results in a successful outcome. Yet we opt for the thinking mind to take control when we're in a pressure situation.

What is it that makes us believe our thinking mind will best get us through a physical challenge, even though we get regular feedback to the contrary? Perhaps we remember all the times as children when we were told, "Be careful. Watch what you're doing. Make sure you do it right. Slow down. Try harder. Don't make a mistake." Unfortunately, those words only made us more fearful and worried, and pretty much guaranteed that we'd mess up. But we talk that way to ourselves, in our lives and on the golf course, and especially when we putt. We get in our own way.

Getting out of our own way first requires recognition of what's interfering with our performance. If we don't know how we're getting in our own way, how do we begin to get out of the way? Recognition requires the perspective to see our attitudes and actions within a framework that offers us choices. Within that framework we can recognize what will give us the best opportunity to accomplish our intention.

What we need to act on falls into two categories: what needs to be cultivated or enhanced, and what needs to be abandoned or refrained from. We need to reinforce and nurture the habits that we seek to cultivate. We need to change or let dissolve the habits we seek to abandon. Reinforcing and changing habits both require mindful awareness of our thoughts and actions so that we can clearly see the way we engage in our activities.

Dr. William Glasser, who developed Reality Therapy, suggests asking a series of four questions that can serve as a framework for recognizing our habitual patterns. We can contemplate four such questions that will help us clarify what habits to reinforce or cultivate and what habits to change. All we need to ask ourselves is: What are we seeking to accomplish? What have we been doing that has served to accomplish it or has interfered with accomplishing it? How well have our habits been working for us? To the extent they have not been effective, what could we do differently?

Changing Habits

A habit is reinforced when a positive feeling accompanies the completion of the habitual action. It is important to associate the positive feeling with the execution of aspects of our process rather than tie it to the result of the shot.

Changing or dissolving a habit is accomplished by giving less attention to the unwanted action and its result. That is easier said than done. Therefore we need a technique for directing our energy away from one habit to let it fade away, while reinforcing a more helpful habit to replace it. When we establish a strong intention to change a particular habit, having a nonjudgmental awareness of when we are engaging or refraining from the habit will move our behavior in the direction of our intention.

For instance, doubt or second-guessing ourselves can cause a last-instant adjustment to our swing as we stroke a putt. The adjustment is an expression of a lack of commitment to our choice of path or pace, an example of getting in our own way that produces poor outcomes. To change that behavior, first we have to recognize that the habit of putting without commitment was the cause of the missed putt. Next we need to establish a strong intention to putt only when we feel committed to our plan. Finally, we stay nonjudgmentally aware of the extent to which we remain committed to each putt through the round. To put this into practice, write the word *Commit* on your scorecard and make a mark, like the letter *C*, for each putt you execute with commitment. Write the letters *LC* for each putt that lacks commitment.

Knowing in the back of our mind that we are making ourselves accountable for our level of commitment after each putt, we will catch ourselves more often before we go ahead and putt without commitment. Over several rounds, the number of times we putt with commitment will increase, and our scores will improve.

It is also important to remember that when you are changing habits, your results will be inconsistent at first. During the process of training yourself to cultivate certain behaviors and abandon others, it is essential to trust your basic abilities and to accept whatever form the temporary results may take.

PRACTICE EXERCISE:

A common habit among amateur golfers is that of leaving putts short. To change this habit, write on a line of your scorecard *Putts Left Short* and make an *S* for every putt that doesn't reach the hole. Give yourself a check mark or star for every putt that rolls at the pace you intended, into the hole or within two feet past it. Without consciously changing the way you putt, you'll soon leave fewer putts short.

The same technique can be applied if you habitually leave your chip shots or your approach shots from the fairway well short of the flagstick.

Whatever the habit, remember that the key elements are (1) to establish a strong intention to change the habit, (2) to make note of each time you realize you did the habitual action, and (3) to be nonjudgmental, just being objectively aware of your actions without engaging in self-criticism. For most golfers, self-criticism itself would be a good example of a habit to change.

Be an Objective Detective

Every putt is a learning opportunity. If the putt went well, we have the opportunity to reinforce our process and deepen the extent to which our routine is consistent and our stroke ingrained. If the putt didn't go well, we can reflect on our swing and our routine, and take measures to improve them. Most importantly, we can reflect on our state of mind before, during, and after the putt. Putting becomes an opportunity to learn more about ourselves and any habitual patterns of thoughts and emotions that get in our way. To learn from every putt, we need to clear whatever emotion arose about the outcome and then examine the evidence like a detective, one who is detached and objective about what is there and what isn't.

The work of such an *objective detective* is to look for clues and learn from them. Find out what you saw in the surface of the green that wasn't there, or what you didn't see that was there. Look for aspects of the lay of the land you may have forgotten to take into account as you read the putt. Then set your intention to learn from the experience and to remember to look for those clues before future putts. In this way you can improve your ability to read greens as you play.

After every putt leaves the putter face, the first thing to reflect on is the quality of your execution. Did you *make* the putt you intended? In other words, independent of how it turned out, did the putt start with a good stroke, on the path that you intended, at the pace that you intended? You know the answer almost immediately after the ball has started on its way.

CASE #1: Making the Putt and Holing the Putt

When you make the putt *and* hole the putt, the result itself provides reinforcement by rewarding you with a better score. Responding to a good result with positive emotion reinforces your process, giving you credit for a job well done. Encourage yourself with statements like, "That's how I putt when I commit to my routine," or "That's how I putt when I get out of my own way." You are telling yourself that your best-quality effort appears naturally when you give yourself the right conditions—commitment and trust in your stroke, path, and pace.

CASE #2: Making the Putt but Not Holing the Putt

You executed the putt you intended, but the ball missed the hole by a significant margin. To be an objective detective, clear any emotional reaction with a full breath, letting it go all the way out. Since you made the putt you intended, you need to look for clues as to why the ball took a very different path than you expected it to.

Look at the lay of the land and the surface of the green for clues about what happened. What didn't you see that was there? Perhaps you neglected to take into account the effect of grain. Alternatively, what did you see that wasn't really there? Maybe you judged a slope to be more severe than it was, and so the putt broke less than you thought it would. This process of investigating putts you *made but didn't hole* is the very best way to improve your green-reading abilities. Make a mental note to pay particular attention on the next putt to what you misjudged on the last one.

CASE #3: Not Making the Putt

If the stroke, path, and/or pace were not as you intended, then you need to find out what got in the way. Isolate what may have interfered with your ability to trust your stroke. What kept you from committing to the path or the pace you chose?

Suspect A: The Stroke

If you felt it wasn't a good stroke, reflect on what might have gotten in the way of swinging the putter like you do when you putt to nowhere. Check your grip pressure.

Suspect B: The Path

A poor stroke could have sent it off on the wrong path. Check back on Suspect A. Lack of commitment could have caused you to push or pull the putt. Commit to your read.

If you felt the stroke was good, most likely you were aimed in a different direction than you thought. Until you have an opportunity to check your aim on the practice green, use an intermediate target a foot or so in front of the ball for alignment.

Suspect C: The Pace

If the stroke was poor, the off center contact or deceleration will result in too slow a pace. Too tight a grip can cause an extra hitting action or a holding back instead of a smooth swing and interfere with feel for pace.

Lack of commitment to the pace you chose could cause you to manipulate the size or speed of the swing while in action. Whether you hold back or give it something extra, there won't likely be a happy ending. Rehearse the stroke you want to make and focus on reproducing it.

If you felt you made a good stroke with just the size of swing you intended, but the ball didn't roll the distance you thought it would, you misjudged how big a stroke you needed to make for the putt. If you have a consistent pattern of misjudgment, spend more time gauging your pace and swing size on the practice green.

Those three cases presenting the combinations of making and holing a putt illustrate the process of being an objective detective and discovering the habitual patterns that keep us from playing our best. Once we recognize these habits, we can apply the technique of combining strong intention and nonjudgmental awareness to clear the interference and get us back on track.

Instead of simply being frustrated at a missed putt, an objective detective treats it as an opportunity to learn. If you apply yourself to practicing this way of responding to results, you'll find it easier to get out of your own way and to continually improve your putting.

Selective Memory

Memory is selective. No one remembers everything that happened in any given moment. There's so much input from all your senses and thoughts that you can't be consciously aware of it all, let alone remember it. So you can be sure that whatever your memories are of an event, that's not entirely what happened.

Your mind chooses to pay attention to what you expect to see, to what matches the way you see your world and yourself. If you are expecting to have trouble off the tee, your mind will see the hazards instead of the fairway. If you're expecting failure on the green, your mind will see the many ways your putt can miss instead of the best path for it to go in the hole.

We bring to the foreground of our minds whatever matches our current experience of our world and ourselves. Getting confirmation that the way we see things is correct is such a high priority that we will ignore or dismiss great amounts of evidence to the contrary. We will pay attention to and exaggerate the importance of even one instance that matches our view of how things are. Because most golfers focus on what goes wrong, it takes a number of rounds of good putting to begin to feel that their putting is great, but it takes just a few badly missed putts to make them certain that their putting is terrible.

Emotions play a big part in the direction and extent to which aspects of our memories are skewed. Emotions give certain memories extra weight, a higher priority in how easily recallable they are. Missing a three-footer on the last hole to lose a tournament will stay in your memory much longer than the three-footer you may have missed on the very same hole in the first round, when the outcome of the tournament was several days away.

You remember most strongly that which gives rise to intense thoughts and emotions during and just after an event. If you focus on what goes well, you'll remember more of those aspects of the event. If you get worked up over what goes wrong, that's what you'll remember.

You can affect the way you selectively remember an event by intentionally directing the energy of emotion. You do so by enthusiastically identifying with the positive aspects of your experience, and detaching yourself from the negative aspects. When you hit a good putt, whether it goes in or not, get excited about how it felt coming off the sweet spot of the putter face, feel good about how it rolled end over end along the path you chose, with just the pace you had in mind.

If the putt wasn't struck well, refrain from beating yourself up about it. You'll see pros tamp down an imaginary bump in the green, rather than taking it personally. The idea is to get into the habit of reacting less emotionally to a poor putt, and instead immediately looking for what interfered with your process. Be more reflective and distant from the experience, giving it less emotional power.

When you roll a putt that goes in just the way you pictured it, feel great about how well you executed your process as well as the result you got. That's the best way to build strong memories of success.

Start Where You Are

The purpose of mental game training is to help us get out of our own way. When we clear the interference that arises from hope and fear, we can consistently play up to our potential. The next step is to enhance our abilities, and raise the level at which we can perform.

As you get better at getting out of your own way, you can improve your capabilities through improved technique. Better technique will contribute to more confidence in your putting and everything else about your game.

To improve your technique, it is essential to be realistic about where you are now. If someone asks you to draw them a map for directions to get somewhere, you not only need to know where they want to go, you need to know where they are when they start. The map won't do them much good unless the starting place they give you is where they are now.

Your starting place is an objective inventory of your strengths and the areas in which you could improve. In describing your starting place, it is helpful to refrain from negativity. The first sentence of this paragraph was an example of that—instead of the word *weaknesses*, I used *areas in which you could improve*. Notice that using the word *could* emphasizes your positive potential for improvement. *Should* is negative and judgmental.

Simply write down, or describe to your instructor, what your putting is like. Make your description as objective and nonjudgmental as possible. Evaluate your skill level for different kinds of putts—short, long, left to right, right to left, uphill, downhill, two tiers, big breakers. Pay attention to your language. Whenever a negative or judgmental image arises, catch it, clear it, and redescribe the situation in a purely objective way.

For example, instead of saying, "I'm terrible at short putts," you can say, "I have room for improvement in my short putting." It may seem like a small matter, but how we describe ourselves affects how we feel about ourselves. Feeling better about yourself gives you more confidence that the work you plan to put in will pay off. Now you can start where you are and set about enhancing your abilities in those areas where you have room for improvement.

Know Your Tendencies

Standing on the practice range at the Masters Tournament with Nick, he got a bit frustrated and jokingly said, "Doc, I've been out here twenty years. When will my hand remember what it's supposed to do?"

I said, "Nick, it never will permanently. We all have tendencies that keep coming back throughout our golfing life. What you need to do is keep a list of yours, recognizing the symptoms in your ball flight patterns or putting that your tendencies produce. Then you'll be able to apply the remedies that have worked in the past to help you play golf at the highest level."

"I used to do that," he said. "I had a list of at least a dozen things."

"Just a few main ones are all you need," I suggested. "The rest will come along. When someone has too long a list of things to check on, they soon don't want to look at it at all."

We all have tendencies that are deeply grooved into our way of playing golf. No adjustment to the action of swinging a club lasts forever. Over time we revert back to familiar tendencies, little by little. The process happens subtly, unnoticed because the changes are in such small increments as to be imperceptible. As they accumulate, we are less and less able to compensate for them, until we are very much off our game.

What can we do to remedy the situation? Keeping a written record of your tendencies is the most efficient and effective way to relate to them. Note the tendencies you have that interfere with your ideal mental game preparation, action, and response to results. Be aware of any unhelpful tendencies in your physical setup as well. Do this as an objective detective, not judging or criticizing yourself. Objectively analyze your patterns, what causes them, and what works best to remedy them.

You can turn your game around as you play if you know your tendencies. You can diagnose symptoms and causes much as a doctor would. Then work with your instructor on the best remedies to get you back on track.

To do this properly, get a small notebook or a few index cards and draw lines to form three columns on a page. At the top of the columns write the words *Symptoms*, *Causes*, and *Remedies*. The *symptoms* are the patterns that show up when your putts or other shots aren't going the way that you intend. Perhaps you're not rolling the ball as well as usual, not making contact on the sweet spot. Notice what the patterns of your misses are. Have your instructor watch you and help you identify the causes. Then work with your instructor to identify the tendencies that cause your particular symptoms, and explore possible remedies to deal with those tendencies.

For example, your pattern may be that you leave a lot of putts short. Check your list of what you do that *causes* that symptom. It may be that the swing path you've developed is creating a glancing impact, not square to where the putter face is aimed. It may be that you're coming up out of the putt, and therefore not making solid contact. For those causes, the *remedies* may include holding your finish and keeping your body steady long after the ball is on its way.

To be prepared for a time when your tendencies reappear, enter the information in the columns on your putting page. In the *Symptoms* column, write *leaving the putt short* and *feeling of poor contact*. In the *Causes* column write *coming up out of the putt*. In the *Remedies* column, write *keeping head and body steady* and *hold the finish*.

It is important to remember that when you're looking for causes, do not look just at the surface cause of that symptom. Every pattern of ball roll or flight will have a physical cause that produces it. But behind every physical cause is a deeper mental game cause. In our example, the tendency to come up out of the putt is a physical cause of off center contact. However, the mental cause behind that action would be overconcern with the results, worry about how the putt is going to turn out, which makes you want to look too soon.

If you know your tendencies, you can recognize them rather quickly, even during a competitive round of golf. If you have your notebook in your bag, you'll be able to make adjustments as you play because you have the information you need to identify the patterns of your symptoms, your tendencies that cause those patterns, and the remedies that reverse those tendencies.

Be Your Own Coach

In most sports, athletes have coaches at every practice and every competition. Not so in golf. Many golf instructors see their students only once a week on the range, and never even go out on the course with them. That's why you need to know how to coach yourself in practice and on the course. The way to do that is to take the role of coach and talk to yourself as if you were another player with the same problem you're facing. Think of what you'd tell the other player, then turn around and coach yourself with the same words.

As a coach, you would objectively analyze the process and results of your student playing a golf shot. Being your own coach means reflecting on your process and the results as part of your post-shot routine to identify patterns and tendencies. Apply the Symptoms/Causes/Remedies system presented in the previous chapter. Recognize patterns of symptoms from your list, reflect on the causes, and apply the remedies.

Being your own coach is a lot like being your own best friend, or being your own caddie during a round of golf. Most players think they don't really know what to say to themselves. Yet I watch them give advice to a partner in a match or help out a buddy by caddying for them in an event. They know exactly what to say and not to say. They know exactly the things that are helpful, and exactly the things to refrain from saying because they aren't helpful. It's ironic that they don't realize they can talk to themselves that way. As I point out in *Zen Golf*, saying something encouraging to a friend who hits a poor shot is easy, but saying it to yourself in the same circumstances is much harder.

All you have to do to be your own coach is to be more ob-jective, to look at the circumstances as if you are an observer rather than the actor. When a challenging situation comes up in which you feel uncertain what to do, just imagine that you're caddying for a player who's facing the exact same shot and think of what you as a good caddie would recommend. You'll be surprised at how many times you come up with the solution that you're searching for, how quickly you find it, and how ap-propriate the solution is. You can't find it from inside the situ-ation, but when you step outside to have a look as an objective observer, it's very evident to you. That's the way to be your own coach.

Give Yourself Permission

Learning a new way of doing things can make you feel nervous, self-conscious, and apprehensive. When you make a change, it may feel different and awkward. My students often say, "That doesn't feel comfortable," and my response is, "What you were doing before was comfortable. How well was comfortable work-ing for you?"

What is familiar is comfortable; what is unfamiliar is often uncomfortable. Part of that feeling comes from concern that we're doing something the wrong way if it doesn't feel right.

To make a change more easily, it's helpful to remember that awkward feelings are part of the learning process. There-fore, the best thing we can do is give ourselves permission to feel awkward. For example, when golfers soften their grip, it often feels uncomfortable. They were used to having a tighter grip, making a little jablike stroke, and hitting at the ball. They weren't used to swinging the putter back very far or through very far. With a softer grip, they need to make a bigger swing, both back and through, to make the ball roll the same distance. When they make a big swing, it feels very strange and fear arises that they're going to hit the ball much too far, as far as they would have if they had taken a big swing *and* hit it as hard as they usually did with their tighter grip.

I let them know the logic of making a bigger swing, and explain that they need to give themselves permission and literally say to themselves, "It's okay if the swing feels bigger than I'm used to. It's okay to make a swing that feels bigger than I'm used to."

It usually takes less time than we think for new movements to become comfortable, as long as we don't struggle with them. I've watched players take two strokes with a left-hand low grip and say, "Oh this is terrible. I can't get comfortable doing this." I tell them that at first most people feel uncomfortable with a new way of holding a putter, and suggest that if they want to make a change, just to stay with it for a while without expectation. After a dozen more putts they start feeling comfortable.

Doing something new will become comfortable more quickly if you give yourself permission for it to feel different from what you're used to. The point is that whatever change you're making will feel strange. If you're doing it as your instructor wants you to, put that feeling into words. Give yourself permission to feel that way by saying, "It's okay if it feels a little too close. It's okay if it feels as if I'm making a bigger swing with the putter. It's okay." That gives you confidence and assures you you're not doing something wrong. You're just doing something a new way, the way you really want to do it, and it's only a matter of time before you get used to it.

Practice Drills
as Remedies

Knowing your tendencies allows you to practice in a way that remedies the symptoms of unhelpful habits. You can strengthen your ability to refrain from certain actions by exaggerating their opposites. For example, if you have a tendency to stand up out of a putt, exaggerate the opposite action: Practice rolling putts without looking to see where each one finishes until well after you've completed your stroke. When Tiger Woods practices putting, he'll roll long putts and not look up to see how they turn out until they are almost to the hole.

Following are other examples of remedying symptoms by exaggerating their opposites and heightening your awareness:

Pushing and Pulling

The tendency to push or pull appears primarily on breaking putts. Develop the remedy for pushing and pulling by heightening your awareness of the feel of your putting-to-nowhere stroke. Notice how your stroke finishes when the putt goes where the putter face was aimed, with an end-over-end roll.

Practice finishing your stroke that way, holding your finish for an extra second or two.

Set up with the putter face aiming along the start of the path you've chosen. Make your putting-to-nowhere stroke as if it were a straight putt, and hold your finish. Practice until you can consistently finish your stroke the same way no matter what size or direction of break you face.

Big Backswing

If your tendency is to take an overly long backswing, it will result in your decelerating or shortening your follow-through. You can remedy that tendency by placing a water bottle behind the ball at the size of swing you want to make for a particular distance. You'll get the feedback immediately if you hit the water bottle. As an additional remedy, apply an exaggeration practice: Roll twenty-one putts in which your follow-through is bigger than your backswing. If a follow-through is too short, start over until you can do twenty-one in a row.

Recoil

At the finish of the forward motion of the putting stroke, some golfers have the tendency to recoil, or bring the putter back quickly toward the center of their stance. This can lead to quickness of tempo and an incomplete follow-through. Remedy this tendency in practice by holding your finish for an exaggerated length of time. Finish the forward stroke and hold the putter in place for a count of three before you move it.

Coming Up Out of the Putt

The tendency to come up out of the putt is a habit caused by anticipation of looking for the result. To remedy this habit, hold your spine angle and posture steady for an exaggerated length of time after the ball leaves the putter face. When you do eventually look to see how the putt finished, do so only by turning your head and not standing up. Practice turning your head to look while holding your posture in place for three putts in a row. Please note that proper posture will prevent your back from getting sore from this practice.

Shortcutting Your Routine

Finally, if you tend to skip sections of your routine or find yourself going through the motions but not really paying careful attention, spend time practicing your routine by doing some of the elements in an exaggerated way. Go through every part of your routine in slow motion to heighten your awareness.

Whenever you recognize patterns arising from unhelpful tendencies, apply the remedies of exaggerating opposite actions and of heightening awareness of the patterns you want for better execution. Practicing in that way will make it easier to use nonjudgmental awareness and intention to change unhelpful habits as you play.

Practice the Way You Play: Structuring Your Practice Session

Start your practice session with a body scan and some rhythmic breathing so that you feel settled and centered. Then practice the drills related to each of the components of a putt: stroke, pace, and path. Finally, practice your full putting routine in the way you'll want to when you play.

Practice Your Posture

Proper putting posture is very helpful for your practice session. Feel the straightness of your spine extending up and forward from the back of your head and down and back from your tailbone. With that posture, it is easy to let your arms swing freely beneath your torso. Attend to your posture in practice and it will become your natural posture when you play. You'll also feel less strain on your back with good posture, allowing you to practice your putting for a longer time without getting tired and sore.

Practice Putting to Nowhere

Always start by practicing your putting-to-nowhere stroke. Go through a routine of first swinging the putter without a ball, then swinging the same way through the ball, then varying the size of swing you make while maintaining the same flow and tempo. Practice until you feel that the sweet spot of the putter face is consistently contacting the ball.

Then practice any other drills connected with the quality of the roll, including any drills you do to combat your unhelpful tendencies, such as the exaggeration practices of keeping your posture steady and holding your finish.

Practice Your Feel for Pace

Next do drills connected with feel for pace. It's a good idea to occasionally check your grip pressure. Squeeze the putter handle as tightly as you can, then hold it as softly as you can. Find your ideal grip pressure by making it just firm enough to feel you have control of the putter.

Practice the "Guessing Game for Feel." Guess out loud if you expect the putt to be long, short, or about right, and then look to see how it turned out. Reflect on the feel that produced that result. Repeat until you are rolling putt after putt near the edge.

In *Zen Golf* I described the "Leapfrog Game for Touch" in putting. You try to roll successive putts past the previous putt by as little as you can, with a penalty for any you leave short. See how many putts you can fit within a set distance from the first putt. Keep trying to improve your best score. It's also a fun game to play as a contest, to practice under competitive pressure.

Practice Reading Putts

Practice reading breaking putts from different distances with different slopes. For each putt, practice gradually playing more and more break, up to the maximum break you can play and still have the ball reach the hole. Through this exercise you'll find the amount of break you're most comfortable playing for different distances and for the severity of the side slope as it gets more extreme. Keep in mind that it's important to conserve mental energy. In other words, it is less stressful to leave a putt six inches short than to face a tough comebacker after you run it six feet past.

Practice Your Routine

Perhaps the most overlooked yet most important thing to practice is your putting routine. Go through your full routine, just as you would in a match. Using one ball, putt to different holes on the practice green from varying distances. Hole out each time, including tap-ins. It may take more time, but you'll be making a very good exchange of quantity for quality. Practice flowing through your routine with regular, rhythmic tempo.

Practice sessions are an opportunity to experiment with different ways of working with your breathing and your practice stroke in your routine. Pay heed not to get sloppy and short-circuit the process, and your routine will serve you better on the course.

Practice the Way You Play

The best putting practice is to practice the way you play—in a competitive situation. Find a friend for putting contests and play for a little something to add to the pressure so that you really feel the competitive edge. It doesn't have to be monetary; you can keep track of your record for bragging rights and even have a little year-end trophy.

You can also have competitions against yourself. Use your best score in a game or contest as your goal to keep improving your putting. See if you can better your record each month, especially on putts of eight feet or less, as those are the ones you may need to save par.

Practicing short putts is an important part of each session. Include drills that bring in some pressure, like putting two-footers from the four directions around a hole, then doing so for three-footers, and so on, having to start over if you miss a putt. See how far in the sequence you get, and with each practice session, see if you can extend your record. Knowing you can hole many short putts in a row will give you an edge in confidence when you face one late in a match.

Summary of a Practice Session

- Connect with your posture; get settled and centered.
- Practice your putting-to-nowhere stroke.
- Practice drills and games to improve your feel for pace.
- Practice your reading skills for judging path and pace on breaking putts.
- Practice your putting routine for flow and tempo.
- Have putting contests to practice the way you play.

PART 8

Golf and Life: Putting Things into Perspective

To be a warrior is to learn to be genuine in every moment of your life.

—Venerable Chögyam Trungpa

The End of the World

During a round of golf, whatever we are making a big deal out of or getting worried about moves to the foreground in our minds, taking up a larger percentage of the landscape of our experience than it deserves to.

If we get caught up in how a putt will turn out, that becomes a big deal, and our interest in quality of execution fades into the background. The concern for results interferes with our connection to the process. We may find ourselves going through the motions of our routine but not really being present for it, because the outcome of the putt is foremost in our mind. If we can shift our focus and take more interest in the process, worrying about the result takes a backseat. We can be fully present in our routine and execute to the best of our ability.

When we play golf, we might be so disappointed after losing a big event that we feel it is the end of the world. Certainly we might think our own demise would qualify even though after we're gone, the rest of the world will go on.

But the only thing that is really and truly the end of the world is . . . the actual end of the world. Anything else is not a big deal in comparison.

This is not meant to minimize the impact of catastrophes and the suffering that accompanies them, which are all too real. It is helpful to remind ourselves of that, to keep things in perspective. Missing a putt, no matter how big a tournament is on the line, is not the end of the world. Take a step back and look at the whole world. You may find that, in the big scheme of things, whether a putt falls or not isn't such a big deal after all.

It Will Pass

A student went to his teacher and said, "I don't know what to do. I am completely terrible at mindful awareness practice. Sometimes my mind is totally wild; sometimes I'm completely drowsy. I'm preoccupied with the past half the time, the future the other half. I can't just be present and relax. I'm completely frustrated, and getting nowhere."

"It will pass," the teacher said, without seeming the least bit concerned.

After a month, the student requested another interview. "You were so right. Now my practice is excellent. I feel very settled and calm, very much aware and present, very relaxed and confident! I'm making great progress."

"It will pass," the teacher said, without seeming the least bit impressed.

Golfers understand the impermanence of success and failure, but we often forget that it applies to ourselves. One day we feel we've found the key to great putting, and we'll never have a bad day on the greens again. Another day we feel completely lost and come to the firm conclusion that we've lost our putting stroke forever. Neither is true. We just take what we're experiencing in the present, forget it was different in the past, and project it out as the only possible future. At that moment we've lost perspective, and gotten caught up in an extreme view.

The remedy that can free you from such an all-or-nothing mentality is to take a step back and recognize that every experience is temporary. Enjoy your success without too much self-congratulation. Work on what you need to improve without getting down on yourself.

When he learned that I coach golfers, one of my meditation teachers told me, "If they understand impermanence and the lack of solidity of their experiences, they won't get too excited when they do well and they won't get too depressed when they do poorly. That way they will be able to keep their minds in the moment and play better."

Not Afraid to Be a Fool

My teacher, Chögyam Trungpa, called this his favorite slogan. It represents complete freedom from self-consciousness. It is the opposite of taking oneself seriously.

Most people take themselves far more seriously than is good for them, or for the people around them. Taking oneself too seriously is an expression of attachment to one's self-image. It betrays an underlying lack of confidence in one's inherent worth as a person. Behind it is usually a need to be seen a particular way by others in order to feel valid.

I was working with a young pro who had qualified for and was playing in a higher-level tournament than those on his regular tour. After a mediocre first round, he said, "Well, at least I didn't embarrass myself out there."

I told him, "If that was your primary motivation, to not embarrass yourself, your time would have been better spent just about anywhere else."

If you are afraid to look like a fool, you'll rarely make a free swing on a long putt, and you'll be terrified of short ones. Not much feels more foolish than missing a two-foot putt. That's the way the yips get started for some people: The very fear of looking like a fool by missing a two-foot putt becomes a self-fulfilling prophecy.

Maintaining a sense of humor about one's foibles is not only healthy but also appreciated by others. Most people prefer the company of those who don't take themselves too seriously. If you're not afraid to be a fool, making a mistake won't embarrass you. If you're not afraid to make a mistake, you'll swing your putter more freely, and you'll always be open to learning something new.

Your attitude has a lot to do with how well you execute a challenging putt. Do you see it as an opportunity to showcase your abilities, or as an obstacle to getting what you want? One approach inspires excitement; the other arouses a feeling of dread. Great players look for opportunities. When the game is on the line, they want the ball in their hands. They are not afraid to take the risk of being a fool if they can have the chance to be the hero.

Stop Should-ing
All Over Yourself

Reflecting on what we should or shouldn't have done in the past and instructing ourselves as to what we should or shouldn't do in the future are such common thoughts that we pay them little heed. Unfortunately, they can actually have a powerful negative impact on our putting and our golf game in general.

Using *should* in your self-talk brings with it feelings of

judgment and negativity. "I *should* have sunk that putt. I *should* have made par on that hole. I *should* hole this putt. I *should* birdie the next hole." Each of those comments adds to the burdens of remorse and worry that interfere with your process and drain your energy.

Anytime you use *should* in reference to a past action, you introduce guilt and blame. Anytime you use *should* in reference to a future result, it adds pressure because it introduces expectation. It also carries with it an implied threat of punishment, a mental add-on that starts with *or else*. "I should make this putt, *or else* I'll feel like a lousy golfer."

Instead of *should*, try using the word *could*. When you substitute *could* for *should*, you are not denying your intention with regard to what happened or will happen. But you are focusing on the positive possibilities instead of the negative consequences.

PRACTICE EXERCISE:

This exercise helps you feel the difference between "should" and "could." Turn the focus of your awareness to your body. Use a settling, clearing breath to dissolve excess tension. Then pay attention to how your body feels when you say the following pairs of sentences, changing only the word *should* to *could*:

"I should have made par on that hole."

"I could have made par on that hole."

One conveys a feeling of criticism; the other leaves open the door for improvement.

Compare the different feelings you have when you say, "I should make this putt," versus "I could make this putt." Notice the difference in your tone of voice and body language as well.

Should adds pressure and carries an *or else* with it, while *could* emphasizes potential and promise.

Change the way you talk to yourself and you *could* find that you are performing better and enjoying yourself more, on the greens and in everything you do.

Making Friends with Yourself

Being a friend means accepting another person for the whole of who they are, the parts we like about them as well as the parts we aren't as fond of. We share in their joy at success, and we offer them support when things aren't going so well. On the other hand, people who are on your side when things are going well but abandon you when you're struggling are just fair-weather friends. Sometimes they'll even turn on you when you don't live up to their expectations. These are not the type of people we want in our lives.

There may be one of those fair-weather friends who spends a lot of time with you. This fair-weather friend has high expectations and gives you a hard time whenever you fall short, is stingy with compliments and generous with criticism. Sound like someone you know? Take a look in the mirror. Most of us treat ourselves as a fair-weather friend would.

One of the most pervasive habits I've observed among golfers is the tendency toward instant self-criticism. No matter how good a shot looks to their fellow competitors, they always seem to be able to find something wrong with it. You say, "Good shot," and they'll immediately tell you why it wasn't.

You may think that if you don't analyze every shot and examine your mistakes, you won't correct them. However, when you focus on what went wrong, you lose the opportunity to reinforce all the things that went right. Positive reinforcement is more beneficial for your continued improvement than punishing yourself for an error.

It's rare that someone compliments himself. Greg Norman used to make it a practice. When he'd hit a putt he really liked, he'd say something to himself like, "Greg, that was a damn good putt. You are a heck of a golfer." That's what a friend would say who is cheering us on. We can give our inner critic a rest and enjoy how good it feels to roll in a long putt.

Tour pros aren't always successful at holing putts, landing drives in fairway, and hitting greens in regulation. Give yourself a break if you're not perfect. The best way to play is to believe in yourself. Fully intend to hit every shot just the way you want to, and at the same time pre-accept a range of results.

When you make friends with yourself, it is easier to be tolerant and accepting of others. When you stop being hard on yourself, it is easier to see how hard others are being on themselves. When you believe in yourself, it is easier to believe in others.

How to Know When a Ball Mark Is Properly Repaired

The answer is simple. You have repaired a ball mark properly when you would be satisfied to putt over it.

Golf is a game of consideration. You can't imagine a golf

tournament in which all the fans of one player would be on the edge of the green, right in the other player's view, waving long balloons and making noise, the way fans do behind the opponent's basket during a free throw in a basketball game. It would also be amazing if a pro basketball player called a foul on himself when the referee didn't see it. Yet professional golfers call penalties on themselves for even an unintentional infraction of the rules.

Respect and thoughtfulness are qualities appreciated by everyone. When given, they are almost universally returned. It's not so complicated to practice. Take a clearing breath before you say or do something, and reflect, "What would I like to hear or receive if I were in that person's place?" Be your own counsel and give yourself the advice you'd give someone else in your position.

Two other qualities that are reflected in golf as a game of honor are honesty and integrity. Here are two simple definitions to keep in mind as guides. Honesty is making your words match the situation. Integrity is making your actions match your words.

If you say you're going to play golf by the rules, moving your ball is lacking integrity, because your actions aren't matching your words. That doesn't mean a club can't have local rules. In fact, it's important that everyone in your group knows them so there aren't misunderstandings about anyone's integrity.

Intentionally reporting fewer strokes on a hole than you actually played is dishonesty. Intention and knowledge are important factors here. Because honesty means making your words match the situation, dishonesty requires that you intentionally communicate or withhold information about something that you know does not reflect the reality of the circumstances.

When doing corporate programs, I often advise the company to add something to their interview procedure for management positions: Take the person out for a round of golf with the people that will be his or her peers. You'll get all the information you need about the character of your prospective colleague. At one corporate program I taught, the CEO said, "We hired someone and in a short time things weren't going well. Then we had our annual company golf tournament. After playing golf with him, those of us in his foursome agreed that if we'd played golf first and done the hiring later, we wouldn't have even considered him."

It's possible that golf builds character.

It's definite that golf reveals character.

With Friends Like These . . .

In football, when the kicker has a field goal to win the game, the opposing coach will call a time-out just before the play is about to start to try to throw the kicker off his rhythm. It's called *freezing the kicker*. The idea is that the kicker will spend the time thinking about the kick, the importance of it, the hope of making it, and the fear of missing it. His thoughts will start to get in his own way. The same thing happens if we have to wait too long before attempting a putt.

A classic example of interference from a fellow competitor happened at the US Open championship in 1949. Just as Sam Snead stepped up to a short putt, his opponent said, "Wait a minute, I think maybe I'm away." They called in the referee who was walking with their group and he measured both putts.

It turned out that Sam was in fact away, if only by an inch. But the other player had used the situation to "freeze" Sam, to throw him off his rhythm and get him thinking about the putt. It worked, because Sam did get in his own way just enough to miss that putt and lose by one stroke.

There are other mind games that show up in golf, some innocent and some intentional. A fellow competitor may use a backhanded compliment to accuse you of being a sandbagger by saying, "You putt awfully well for someone with that high a handicap." If you buy into it, you might feel guilty and start three-putting. A golfer may try to jinx his opponent by telling his partner in an overly loud voice, "This guy has such a great stroke; he always makes these." If you buy into it, you might become preoccupied with technique and miss a simple putt. A well-meaning playing partner might inform you, "Did you know this putt is for a seventy-nine?" That's the innocent version, someone thinking they are being helpful.

There are countless ways to be distracted; it is up to you how you respond to each of them. The remedy for distracting comments is to let them come and go. You can't pretend you didn't hear them. Recognize the thoughts and feelings they bring up, then let them pass on like clouds passing by in the sky.

Whatever mind games you encounter, and however you choose to respond to them, maintaining your own peace and compassion is the key. Be polite but not reactive. Make your own enjoyment of the game your reference point, not how to return what others are dishing out.

Rather than getting angry and letting it upset your game, tune into your breathing to keep your emotions settled and your thoughts in perspective. There's a saying that getting swept away by anger is like reaching into a fireplace to throw hot embers at your enemy. You may hit them or you may not, but you will definitely get burned.

Regard their actions with a feeling of compassion. Sympathy will do more good than anger.

Respond Rather
than React

In the Serenity Prayer, one asks for the courage to control what one can, the serenity to accept what one can't control, and the wisdom to know the difference between the two. You have control over how you execute your putt. You don't have control over the result. You do have control over how you *respond* to the result.

In most circumstances, we will have limited control over what happens to us. However, if our minds are well trained, we can have a good deal of control over the way we respond. Awareness allows you the space to respond out of choice rather than react out of impulse.

If your confidence is based on quality of execution rather than whether or not the putt goes in, you have a better chance of choosing how to respond to the results. What happens to you has less impact on your life than how you respond to what happens to you.

Zen Putting is intended to help you use your mind to improve your putting and golf game. It is also designed to enable you to use your experience in putting and golf to improve your mind.

If you're open to feedback, the moment after impact of any

golf shot instantly reveals everything about your state of mind. After you swing a driver, play an approach shot, or stroke a putt, reflect in an objective way about what thoughts, perceptions, and emotions arose in your mind.

Were you clear, committed, and composed, or were you not fully prepared? Were you concerned about your quality of execution or caught up in hope and fear about results? Were you more concerned with your own experience or with impressing others? Contemplate what you learned, and see if any of these patterns appear as mental habits in everyday life as well. When you recognize habits of thinking and reacting that are unhelpful, you can choose to change them. Through patience and perseverance, with strong intention and mindful attention, what you learn on the putting green can make a difference in your life.

Never Give Up, Never Give In

Kanjuro Shibata Sensei, a living treasure of Japan, is the twentieth in the line of official archers and bowmakers for the emperor. He is the recognized master and most revered instructor of *kyudo*, the martial art of Zen archery. Through his presence, he manifests the essence of warriorship, transmitting the Way of the Bow as a powerful vehicle for cultivating mindful awareness. When studying kyudo with him, students receive training in general conduct that serves as the foundation of all martial arts practices. He gives instruction in the three basic points of the Samurai Code:

Listen

Free yourself from thinking, "What's in it for me?" Then you can genuinely listen to the needs and concerns of others, understanding them on their own terms, not filtered through your personal biases.

Help

Extend your time and energy in service of those in need. Through listening, recognize what they actually need from their experience rather than your ideas of what you think would be good for them. If you see something you think they do not see, show them in a way that helps them recognize it for themselves. Help that is conveyed as an imposition is not an expression of compassion but one of aggression.

Never Give Up

Be tireless in your commitment to your own development and to helping others experience their lives with genuineness and decency. My meditation teacher, Ösel Tendzin, elaborated on this last point, telling his students: "Never give in to feelings of self-doubt and pettiness nor of arrogance and resentment. Never give up on the inherent basic goodness and self-worth of yourself and others."

These principles are a guide to authentic conduct that will benefit you in any circumstance. They can help to clear the interference you may carry with you on the golf course. Keeping them in your heart will help you get out of your own way, allowing your potential to be realized and your best game to show up time after time, in golf and in life.

Beyond Hope and Fear

In putting, in golf, and in everything else we do, we have choices. The most fundamental choices involve the way we see our world, where we direct our energy, and how we respond to our experiences. As our awareness increases, the scope of choices available to us expands beyond what we previously thought possible.

It is possible to choose to encounter our world beyond the reference points of hope and fear.

We go beyond hope and fear when our reference point for confidence is an unconditional belief in ourselves rather than how well we've putted lately. When we have a big perspective and realistic expectations, it is easier to maintain our sense of humor and not take ourselves too seriously.

We go beyond hope and fear when our reference point for success is the quality of execution of the putt rather than how it eventually turns out. We can perform our best when we commit to our process, pre-accept the range of possible outcomes, and free ourselves from worry about results.

We go beyond hope and fear when our reference point for satisfaction is playing golf rather than doing math. How each putt feels coming off the putter face can be the basis of how good a time we're having rather than the numbers we write on the scorecard.

We go beyond hope and fear when our reference point for enjoyment is how the journey feels while we're traveling, rather than whether or not we reach our goal. We can tune in to how good it feels just to play the game: teeing off, approaching the green, swinging the putter, and sending the ball rolling toward the hole. Then doing it all over again.

It is my hope that this book has helped you connect with the joy that comes from putting, playing, and living with confidence and freedom. I hope it has helped you get out of your own way and free you from whatever keeps you from performing your best on the putting green and elsewhere in golf and life. It is my wish that you be able to use what you learn here to gain access to your ultimate potential and capabilities, to feel you can make every putt, and to live your life to the fullest with confidence, dignity, and delight.

INDEX OF EXERCISES

REFERENCES AND
RECOMMENDED READING

Beck, Charlotte Joko. *Everyday Zen*. New York: HarperCollins, 1989.

Burke, Jack. *The Natural Way to Better Golf*. New York: Hanover House, 1954.

Chödrön, Pema. *Start Where You Are*. Boston: Shambhala, 1994.

Farnsworth, Craig. *See It and Sink It*. New York: HarperCollins, 1997.

Gallwey, W. Timothy, *The Inner Game of Golf*. New York: Random House, 1981.

Glasser, William. *Reality Therapy*. New York: Harper Paperbacks, 1989.

Hanh, Thich Nhat. *The Miracle of Mindfulness*. Boston: Beacon Press, 1975.

Hanh, Thich Nhat. *Peace is Every Step*. New York: Bantam, 1991.

Haultain, Arnold. *The Mystery of Golf*. Boston: Houghton Mifflin, 2000 (reprint of 1908 original).

Herrigel, Eugen. *Zen in the Art of Archery*. New York: Pantheon Books, 1953.

Jackson, Phil. *Sacred Hoops*. New York: Hyperion, 1995.

Jones, Bobby. *Golf is My Game*. London: Chatto and Windus, 1962.

Kabat-Zinn, Jon. *Wherever You Go, There You Are*. New York: Hyperion, 1994.

Leonard, George. *Mastery*. New York: Plume, 1992.

Morrison, Alex. *Better Golf Without Pratice*. New York: Simon and Schuster, 1940.

Murphy, Michael. *Golf in the Kingdom*. New York: The Viking Press, 1972.

Nicklaus, Jack. *Golf My Way*. New York: Simon and Schuster, 1974.

Nicklaus, Jack. *Jack Nicklaus' Playing Lessons*. Trumbull (CT): Golf Digest Books, 1981.

Parent, Joseph. *Zen Golf: Mastering the Mental Game*. New York: Doubleday, 2002.

Pelz, Dave. *Dave Pelz's Putting Bible*. New York: Doubleday, 2000.

Penick, Harvey. *The Wisdom of Harvey Penick* [collected writings]. New York: Simon and Schuster, 1997.

Reps, Paul and Nyogen Senzaki. *Zen Flesh, Zen Bones*. Boston: Tuttle Publishing, 1957.

Shoemaker, Fred. *Extraordinary Golf*. New York: G. P. Putnam's Sons, 1996.

Shibata, Kanjuro. *Ryukyu Kyudojo Kun*. Boulder: Zenko International, 2001.

Suzuki, Shunryu. *Zen Mind, Beginner's Mind*. New York: Weatherhill, 1970.

Tendzin, Ösel. *Buddha in the Palm of Your Hand*. Boston: Shambhala, 1982.

Tendzin, Ösel. *Space, Time and Energy*. Ojai: Satdharma, 2004.

Trungpa, Chögyam. *Shambhala: The Sacred Path of the Warrior*. Boston: Shambhala, 1984.

Trungpa, Chögyam. *Great Eastern Sun*. Boston: Shambhala, 1999.

Wodehouse, P.G. *The Golf Omnibus*. New York: Wing Books, 1973.

Woods, Tiger. *How I Play Golf*. New York: Warner Books, 2001.

ABOUT THE AUTHOR

Dr. Joe Parent has coached the mental game in golf, business, and life for three decades. He has a Ph.D. in psychology from the University of Colorado, has studied, practiced, and taught mindful-awareness techniques and philosophy in the Buddhist tradition for over thirty years, and has played golf since he was a teenager. A distinguished PGA Tour instructor, he has attracted golfers ranging from the best in the world to beginners, from celebrities to corporate executives to juniors. Many a club champion has thanked Dr. Joe for getting them to the top.

His first book, *Zen Golf: Mastering the Mental Game*, was published in 2002, quickly rising to the top of the list as the bestselling instructional golf book in America. It is an international sensation, translated into many different languages.

A highly regarded keynote speaker at corporate, celebrity, and charity events nationwide and overseas, Dr. Joe's many media appearances include television, radio, newspapers, and magazines. *Golf Digest* featured Dr. Joe in their popular instructional section "Breaking 100—90—80 and 70." He is on their list of "Top Ten Mental Game Experts" in the world.

Dr. Joe teaches in Southern California at the Ojai Valley Inn and Spa Resort and at The Los Angeles Country Club.

CONTACT INFORMATION

Dr. Joe Parent offers private lessons
and custom golf programs
at the beautiful Ojai Valley Inn and Spa,
a five-star resort in a hidden mountain valley
ninety miles northwest of Los Angeles, California.

For information on
corporate keynote speaking, private lessons,
custom golf schools, and tournament coaching,
as well as audio, video,
and online instructional materials,
please visit
www.ZenGolf.com.
E-mail: Info@ZenGolf.com
Telephone: 805.640.1046
or call toll free: 888.874.9928